WHAT
THIS
AWL
MEANS

WHAT
THIS
AWL
MEANS

Feminist Archaeology at a
Wahpeton Dakota Village

Janet D. Spector

With essential contributions by
Chris C. Cavender, Diane M. Stolen,
Mary K. Whelan, and Randall M. Withrow

MINNESOTA HISTORICAL SOCIETY PRESS

www.mhspress.org

The Minnesota Historical Society Press is a member
of the Association of American University Presses.

International Standard Book Number:
ISBN 13   978-0-87351-278-7
ISBN 10   0-87351-278-2

Printed in Canada
10   9   8   7   6   5

♾ The paper used in this publication meets the minimum requirements of the American National Standard for Information Sciences—Permanence for Printed Library Materials, ANSI Z39.48–1984.

Library of Congress Cataloging-in-Publication Data:

Spector, Janet.
    What this awl means: feminist archaeology at a Wahpeton Dakota village /
Janet D. Spector.
        p.   cm.
    Includes bibliographical references and index.
    ISBN 0-87351-278-2 (pbk.)
    1. Little Rapids Site (Minn.).
    2. Wahpeton Indians—Antiquities.
    3. Wahpeton Indians—Women.
    4. Feminist criticism.
    I. Title.
E99.W135S64   1993
977.6'54—dc20
                                                            92-46737

This book is dedicated
    with love to the memory and
    the spirit of my mother,
    Harriet Dizon Spector
    (1916–1982).

ACKNOWLEDGMENTS

This project has been full of wonder since it began more than a decade ago, in large part because so many people have contributed so much to it in so many different ways. Students and faculty who worked with me at Little Rapids were a constant source of stimulation, encouragement, and insight. I am grateful for my circle of close friends and colleagues who listened patiently, read well, and challenged me with just the right mix of criticism and care. I particularly want to thank Robin Berry, Susan Cahn, Sharon Doherty, Sara Evans, Susan Geiger, Allen Isaacman, Barbara Laslett, Patricia Mullen, Barbara Noble, Elizabeth Scott, Diane Stolen, Denise Tabet, Anne Truax, Gwen Walker, Judith Wanhala, Kath Weston, Mary Whelan, and Randy Withrow for their ever-steady support.

Members of my family—Jess, Nate, Bob, two Susans, Sandy, Rich, David, and Travis—provided nourishing love over this long process. Members of Mazomani's family—Chris, Audrey, Angie, Lorraine, Gary, and Elsie Cavender and Carrie Schommer—have enriched my work and my life. (Elsie Cavender died February 1, 1993, at age eighty-six.)

Jerome Kyllo generously adapted a building on his farm for use as our field laboratory each summer. Paul Klammer and Arlo Hasse shared their precious collections with us. The University of Minnesota graduate school, summer school program, College of Liberal Arts honors program, and the Educational Development Program provided critically needed financial resources for our field and lab work. Terri Valois and Marj Breeden of the anthropology department and Bill Weir and Chuck Kartak of the Minnesota Department of Natural Resources supplied vital logistical support at the university and at the site. Special thanks also to Christy Caine and Barbara O'Connell of the state archaeologist's office for their strategic assistance.

My good fortune continued during the latest phase of this project in working with outstanding editors at the Minnesota Historical Society Press. Ann Regan and Marilyn Ziebarth read with laser-like precision and asked hard questions, all the while treating me and my words with great care and respect. Their engagement, encouragement, and enthusiasm has been a constant source of energy. Finally, I want to thank Karen Miller for keeping me close to the spirit of Little Rapids and Susan Geiger for—among so many things—simply being there.

CONTENTS

WHAT
THIS
AWL
MEANS

ARCHAEOLOGY
AND
EMPATHY

W HEN I EXCAVATE sites and touch things that have lain un-
touched for centuries, I know why I am an archaeologist. But
until now, when I wrote about those sites and objects, I felt no connection with the past, my own or that of the people whose cultural
landscapes I had unearthed. Writing "What This Awl Means," a story
about a Dakota girl who lost a carved awl handle a century and a half
ago, brought back thoughts and feelings I had experienced as a young
girl drawn to archaeology. As I learned about the discipline—and,
especially, how to write about archaeology for academic readers—I
found myself increasingly distanced from the question that had fascinated
me since childhood: What was life like for people in the past? While
composing the awl story in place of the standard archaeological report
or scholarly article, I was reminded of my original reasons for wanting
to be an archaeologist. These motives are empathetic—a longing to
discover essences, images, and feelings of the past—not detached, distanced, objective.

It took me a long time to reconnect with the past. My interests
in archaeology and Indians began in the late 1940s in Madison, Wisconsin, when my grandfather walked with me and my friends to the zoo
in Henry Vilas Park. Our route took us through unmarked Indian burial
mounds on a ridge above the park. I do not recall his ever telling us
anything about the mounds or the people who built them. I doubt

that my grandfather, who had fled Russia around 1890 to escape pogroms against Jewish people, knew anything about Indians, though his experiences with persecution were not so different from theirs. I knew virtually nothing about the Indian mounds except that they were an important, memorable part of my early sense of place.

When I was five, we moved to a Madison neighborhood called Nakoma. We lived on the corner of Cherokee Drive and Shawnee Pass. Almost every street had a real or made-up Indian name: Manitou Way, Waban Hill, Hiawatha Drive, Seminole Highway, Iroquois Drive, Huron Hill. No teachers at Nakoma Elementary School or Cherokee Junior High School thought to tell us how these place-names were selected, let alone anything about the peoples we knew of in this peculiar way.

I remember walking down Cherokee Drive on trash pick-up day and looking in cans to see what broken appliances, gadgets, and other interesting junk neighbors had thrown away. I also liked to scavenge for objects lost in the dry creek near Cherokee Drive. Kids often went to the creek for smoking or other forbidden acts, and sometimes I found clues to children's secrets: a jackknife or a cigarette lighter.

I trace the roots of my interest in archaeology to these childhood wanderings among Indian mounds and along streets bearing Indian names in search of things that people abandoned or lost. Of course the peoples named Huron, Seminole, Iroquois, Cherokee, or Shawnee —groups separated by culture, language, and hundreds of miles when they first encountered Euro-Americans—never lived in my neighborhood or even in Wisconsin. No one ever told me about them or their histories, but I wondered what life was like when other Indian peoples lived in my neighborhood.

I began studying archaeology in 1962 as a freshman at the University of Wisconsin at Madison, but I found the subject much less interesting than I had expected. This disappointed me, since I had decided in the ninth grade to become an archaeologist, despite having been told that girls could not be archaeologists and not knowing what it took to become one. With a few exceptions the readings in undergraduate courses bored me. I despised being required to memorize the esoteric names and obscure traits that defined types of stone tools and pottery. These types constituted the "archaeological cultures" that students dutifully charted through time and space on their final exams. I learned from these courses that archaeologists apparently considered artifact classification more important than the people who had made the tools, about whom very little was said. The archaeology I was taught was objective, object oriented, and objectifying.

Fortunately, in the summer after my sophomore year and throughout my undergraduate years, I had the opportunity to do fieldwork under the supervision of Joan Freeman, an archaeologist for the Wisconsin Historical Society. At the time, women field directors were as unusual as opportunities for women students. I went on my first "dig" in 1964. After a few weeks of practice, we began excavating a site in southern Wisconsin, inappropriately named "Aztalan" by early nineteenth-century observers. They believed that the site's sophisticated remains could not have been left by local Indian people, and they concluded erroneously that Aztecs or colonists from Mexico at one time occupied Wisconsin (Freeman 1986, 355).

Aztalan refueled my interest in archaeology. I remember sitting at the top of a huge, reconstructed earthen temple mound, one of several sacred places at the site, watching a thunderstorm approach. Filled with awe, I ached to know about the Indian people who had built this impressive place several centuries earlier and had left it long before Euro-Americans arrived in the area. I had no idea how or why the Indians built the pyramid, what they did there, or how they explained thunderstorms. Questions like these drifted through my mind as I worked.

For almost a decade of summers I excavated at Indian sites in Wisconsin. At each I imagined being transported into the past and through the empathetic barrier that separated me from the people who once used the broken tools, ornaments, containers, and plant and animal remains we carefully exposed with our trowels. I knew that their world was very different, but I had no framework for understanding it, just the intense wish to know about their perspectives and perceptions.

Neither professors of archaeology nor authors of archaeology texts suggested that we might get closer to these people by studying contemporary Indian languages, religions, or philosophies. They implied that too much time had elapsed, too much change had occurred, too much history separated people from their pasts. People occupied these "prehistoric" sites long before traditional Indian culture had "disintegrated" through contact with Europeans. Contemporary Indians were disconnected from their ancestors. But no one I knew ever bothered to ask Indian people about these notions.

As my training in archaeology progressed, I learned to locate, excavate, and map sites; to record and report findings; to wash, sort, and classify artifacts; and to extract tiny snails, bones, and plant remains from soil samples collected in the field. These techniques, my instructors urged, would inform us about people and their environments. I also learned never to use the word "I" in writing archaeology, because inserting oneself into the picture was either unscientific or unscholarly—I do not remember which.

Reluctantly, I set out to do my master's thesis on the uses of seed analysis in archaeology. I spent months hovering over a microscope and extracting tiny seeds from soil samples collected at an Indian site near Milwaukee that had yielded only sparse cultural remains. I wrote very objectively about my methods of seed recovery, identification, and analysis. I suggested how archaeologists might determine whether the seeds reflected the subsistence practices of the original people living at the site, simply came from plants that once grew there, or had recently worked their way into the soil from temperature changes or earthworm tunneling.

Soon after completing my thesis (Spector 1970) and becoming involved in the antiwar and feminist movements of the late 1960s, I felt so alienated from this kind of archaeology that I left graduate school. Seed analysis was too far removed from anything in the world I cared about.

Working with several graduate students and a professor from the university's anthropology department, I spent the next year creating and teaching in a free school for junior and senior high school students. My interests in archaeology were renewed as I took students to dig in the dump of a nineteenth-century shot-making tower built by early Wisconsin settlers in what is now Tower Hill State Park near Spring Green. Some of the students had been so estranged from traditional schools that they had literally stopped reading and writing, but they loved excavating, mapping, and recording their finds and then investigating them in the library.[1] The students' fascination and delight in archaeology reminded me of my early enthusiasm for it.

Not wanting to lose our momentum after the shot-tower investigation, I designed another archaeological expedition. Drawing on

1. The State Historical Society of Wisconsin in Madison holds the artifacts and site notes.

information about midwestern Indian sites occupied before contact with Europeans, I produced an archaeological map and artifact inventory of an idealized, though not unrealistic, Indian encampment. Then I asked students to interpret what they thought happened there on the basis of the things I "planted" at the site. Creating this puzzle was challenging and rewarding for me, and, once again, previously apathetic students worked energetically as archaeologists, this time developing pictures of the past from the maps and material clues created for them.

In 1971 I returned to graduate school to pursue a doctoral degree. I supported myself by producing a multimedia archaeology curriculum unit based on the free-school experiment (Spector 1974). It was marketed to public schools by a company that produced plastic replicas of everything from human hearts to food products as well as replicas of Indian artifacts. This project, combined with my experience teaching in the school, influenced my development as an archaeologist. They allowed me to experiment with ways to stimulate, rather than suppress, students' imaginative thinking about the past and to write about archaeology for nonacademic audiences.

Inspired by a graduate seminar in ethnohistorical archaeology, I decided to write an ethnohistorical and archaeological study of Wisconsin's Winnebago people for my doctoral dissertation. This was a significant departure from seed analysis, and the prospect intrigued me. Pre-European contact Indian sites—commonly referred to as "prehistoric," a troubling notion implying the existence of a time before history begins—have no associated written documents. "Historic" or post-European contact sites do. This vastly increases the amount of information available for study.

Importantly, however, the two sources are quite different. Physical sites and artifacts represent the only records created by indigenous peoples. Written documents come almost exclusively from non-Indian men whose perspectives on Indian cultures reflect Euro-American politics, practices, and beliefs. Both kinds of records are artifacts, products of specific times and cultures.

My doctoral research was supported by two fellowships: a National Science Foundation award for archaeology dissertations and a Ford Foundation award for research on United States ethnic groups. These grants funded my research, excavations, and analysis of materials from Crabapple Point, a nineteenth-century Winnebago site on Lake Koshkonong in southern Wisconsin. Although I welcomed the funding, my response to the two awards differed.

The science foundation fellowship for archaeology seemed appropriate, but I doubted my credentials in ethnic studies and lacked confidence that the research would contribute much insight into nineteenth-century Winnebago people or their contemporary descendants. I did not know their language and had no plans to work directly with them, although many still live in Wisconsin. In fact, as my research proceeded, my apprehensions about encountering Winnebago people on the dig or at the university increased. Something was very wrong.

Compared with seed analysis, however, this kind of archaeology engaged me. I felt some connection to the Winnebago when handling the fragments of their belongings, things they, too, had handled at Crabapple Point. But I had limited knowledge of their culture and was uneasy about studying them without ever speaking to the descendants of the people who might have lived at or near the site.

After spending several months excavating a small area, I turned to the available literature about historic-sites archaeology to help analyze what we had found. These sources emphasized topics such as where glass trade beads were made and how they were distributed, what types of gunflints and other European trade goods could be used to date sites or mark the appearance of new European regimes, and when traders introduced silver jewelry (Spector 1975).

At this time in the 1960s and early 1970s, historical archaeologists, like prehistoric archaeologists, focused primarily on artifact classification and dating, although their work emphasized European-made artifacts produced for Indians rather than Indian-made artifacts studied by "prehistorians." Historical archaeologists knew more about the intended use of many of the artifacts they found—although not necessarily about how Indians actually used them. Some archaeologists also assumed that they could measure the impact of European culture on native peoples by evaluating how many Euro-American objects such as iron kettles or muskets the Indians had adopted (Quimby 1966). Historical archaeologists rarely looked at Indian responses or resistance to European expansion and domination. They seldom noted that in the face of extended physical and cultural assaults, many Indian people continued, and continue, to live in culturally distinctive communities with direct links to the historic sites that the archaeologists examined.

In 1973 I joined the anthropology faculty at the University of Minnesota. Instead of launching a new field project, I decided to try to develop a feminist approach to archaeology. The emergence of the women's movement and its academic wing, feminist scholarship, had been a critical turning point for me. Feminist criticism had helped explain my dissatisfaction with undergraduate archaeology courses and texts. Not only were they object centered; they were male centered. If people were mentioned at all, they were men. Courses and texts conveyed the impression that most archaeological remains—except pots—were manufactured and used by men, who protected and provided for invisible, but presumably dependent, women and children.

Androcentric or male-centered scholarship was not unique to archaeology or to the University of Wisconsin. Scholars in many fields in the early 1970s had begun laying bare the ramifications of academic scholarship produced almost exclusively by white, middle-class men from Euro-American societies that discriminate on the basis of sex, race, and class. These critics showed that who we are—our gender, cultural background, social and economic position, and personal histories—shapes the character of our scholarly work in significant if often unacknowledged ways. They further demonstrated how women's perceptions and experiences are frequently ignored, trivialized, or peripheralized. They showed that studies about "Man" are not about all humans, as claimed, but about males, and that generalizing from this biased perspective produces inaccurate views of human social life (Minnich 1982).

Archaeology, I found, proved to be no exception. In the late 1970s I worked with Margaret W. Conkey, a colleague at the State University of New York–Binghampton, to explore the impact of androcentric thinking on archaeology (Conkey and Spector 1984; Spector and Whelan 1989). We showed that although archaeologists have never claimed to understand gender roles or relationships based on the remains excavated at archaeological sites, archaeological writings nonetheless contain many assumptions, assertions, and statements of "fact" about gender.

Our study identified a series of stereotypes about the roles and capabilities of men and women. First, archaeological writings typically give far more attention and importance to men and presumed male activities than to women and their presumed activities. Second, these writings portray women as dependent and tethered to domestic duties because of pregnancy, childbirth, and nursing, while men are characterized as independent and capable of making decisions in the public domain. Archaeological writings also tend to assume a rigid sexual division of labor throughout much of prehistory: men hunted and women gathered. This leads researchers to link certain tools to one sex or the other—stone projectile points with men, pottery with women, for example—regardless of the culture being investigated. Third, archaeological writings frequently imply that the male-headed nuclear family organization has been a universal norm since humans first emerged several million years ago, not just in the modern Western world.

By uncritically projecting such stereotypes onto the past, we argued, archaeologists have perpetuated and reinforced culturally specific biases that claim men belong in the important public sector and women in the secondary private sphere. The archaeologists' writings make hierarchical gender arrangements seem immutable, as if they were innate characteristics such as erect posture or the capacity for toolmaking. Finally, they imply that political activities to redress inequalities between men's and women's economic and social power must be futile. Current anthropological studies, of course, prove these ideas to be erroneous. Gender roles, relations, and beliefs, like most other aspects of culture, vary widely and frequently change over time (H. Moore 1988; Morgen 1989).

During the time that Conkey and I prepared our feminist critique of archaeological writings and teaching, I worked on another feminist project with students at the University of Minnesota to develop an archaeological approach to the study of gender (Spector 1983). First we raised a series of questions about possible connections between the material and the nonmaterial dimensions of gender. How do various cultures use material things such as tools, clothing, ornaments, and decorations to signify differences between men and women? How do the activities of male and female adults and children affect the physical layout of their working and living spaces and their communities? How do objects reflect and reinforce gender-based differences in power or status? How are objects used to socialize children about culturally appropriate male or female roles?

Turning specifically to the archaeologist's task of excavating places previously occupied by human groups, we wondered how male and female roles, beliefs, and social interactions might be represented and preserved at sites. How would we know if both men and women had been at the site, or what they did there, or whether women as a group had more, less, or equal power compared to men as a group? Given the cultural and time differences between archaeologists and the people we study, we considered whether we would be able to recognize and interpret archaeological expressions of such gender-specific questions. Yet addressing these questions seemed essential to replacing the old generalizations about the past.

Using historical and ethnographic sources about four different North American Indian groups and drawing on concepts emerging in feminist anthropology, we developed a "task differentiation approach" for studying the archaeology of gender. On a task-by-task basis, we examined male and female activities associated with acquiring and processing food; making and repairing tools, clothing, and buildings; and maintaining effective social relations. We focused on who performed each task; where, when, and how frequently it was done; and what artifacts, structures, and facilities were associated with it. We assumed that what people did and how they related to each other shaped the character of the place they occupied (Schiffer 1976).

Our initial studies were promising. Even though the traditional ethnographic sources were often androcentric and incomplete, our detailed analysis of each group's activities illuminated subtle and important differences in divisions of labor by gender. Our approach challenged orthodox notions about hunting, food gathering, farming, and child care, for example, which archaeologists have often treated as single, indivisible actions rather than multitask activities organized in various ways. Our task analysis also showed how men and women might have responded differently to changes in their natural or social environments depending on the tasks they performed, when they did them, and where they lived. For example, the impact of the fur trade on Winnebago and Dakota men and women must have differed depending on which gender traditionally prepared skins for exchange and conducted the trade, and whose daily activities were most significantly affected by the introduction of new raw materials, tools, and ornaments.

Although our ethnohistoric research intrigued us, it could not tell us how a group's unique arrangement of tasks would be expressed archaeologically. This demanded some information from actual sites. In the summer of 1979, I began searching for a local site that might provide a case study. My plan was to look at the activities of a group of men and women—first by examining written records and then by excavating a site—to see how imperishable remains reflected or did not reflect their task patterns.

The Little Rapids site located near Jordan, Minnesota, about forty-five miles southwest of the University of Minnesota's Minneapolis campus, seemed like a good prospect. Professional archaeologists had never excavated the site, called by the Dakota "Inyan Ceyaka Atonwan" (Village at the Rapids) for a small set of nearby rapids on the Minnesota River.[2] Amateur archaeologists, however, had dug there for decades (Wilford 1941, 1951, 1952, 1956, 1957; UM 1975, MHS 1977). Although I knew little about the documentary or archaeological records, I knew that the site had been occupied by the Eastern Dakota, or Sioux, and that it dated to the early and middle 1800s. Captain Seth Eastman, an artist stationed at Fort Snelling in 1830–31 and again from 1841 to 1848, had sketched and painted detailed scenes of Dakota life, leaving an invaluable visual record of the people and their customs. Because Little Rapids was close to the university, it would be easily accessible for our summer archaeology field program.

We began fieldwork at Little Rapids in the summer of 1980, after securing permission from the state archaeologist and the new landowner, the Minnesota Department of Natural Resources. Before excavating I also sent a description of the project to the state's Indian Affairs Intertribal Board (now the Minnesota Indian Affairs Council). This felt risky. I had no idea what kind of reaction to expect from Indian people, never having consulted with them before on a project. Within a few weeks, Donald G. Gurnoe, the board's executive director, sent me a copy of his letter to Norman Crooks, then chairman of the Prior Lake Sioux Community, the Dakota community closest to Little Rapids.[3] "Many times in the past," Gurnoe wrote, "the scientific community has run afoul of Indian people through failure to communicate and their insensitive approach to the concerns of the community. This, apparently, is not the case in respect to this project, as

2. The spelling Inyan Ceyaka Atonwan follows Riggs's *Dakota Grammar, Texts, and Ethnography* (1893, 159). An alternate spelling for the word village is *otonwe* (Riggs 1890, 389; Williamson [1902] 1970, 254).

3. The other three Minnesota Dakota communities are Upper Sioux at Granite Falls, Lower Sioux at Morton and Redwood Falls, and Prairie Island at Prairie Island, Welch, and Red Wing.

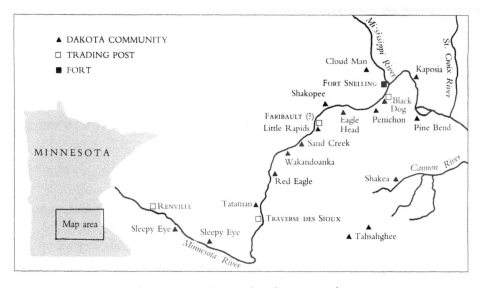

FIG. I. Dakota communities and trading posts, about 1830

Professor Spector has made every effort to enlist the support of Indian people through our offices" (Gurnoe to Crooks, April 7, 1980).

Encouraged and more than a little relieved by this response to my proposal, I tried to reach Chris C. Cavender, a Dakota educator and member of the Upper Sioux Community in western Minnesota, who was recommended to me as a resource person. He was unavailable at the time.

For the next three summers, I directed the archaeology field school at Little Rapids. During 1980 and 1981, we excavated portions of the Dakota encampment. In the 1982 season, we sampled an area several hundred feet to the north that amateur archaeologists in the 1930s and 1940s had identified as a fur trading post (Klammer and Klammer 1949). Then we suspended our excavations in order to analyze the materials we had recovered.

Because Little Rapids was the only nineteenth-century Eastern Dakota site in Minnesota that archaeologists had systematically excavated, we could not compare our finds with those at any nearby sites. Numerous Dakota communities existed in the area until the 1850s, however, when the Dakota officially ceded their lands to the United States government and relocated westward (FIG. I). These communities would have been associated with one of the seven Dakota council fires, or Oceti Sakowin, words meaning leagued or allied. Included were the Mdewakanton, Sisseton, Wahpekute, and Wahpeton Dakota, known collectively as the Eastern Dakota (Riggs 1893, 158; Cavender 1986). Little Rapids was one of several Wahpeton villages. The other three Oceti Sakowin—the Yanktonais, Yankton, and Teton, known collectively as the Western Dakota—lived in villages farther west in the nineteenth century (Riggs 1893, 156–64; Black Thunder 1975, 98; Babcock 1945; and Pond [1908] 1986).

My first publication about our work at Little Rapids tried to link tasks that had been described in nineteenth-century documentary sources—for example, those associated with raising corn, hunting deer, and preparing hides—with physical materials from hypothetical activity areas (Spector 1985). By examining how the Dakota organized tasks, when and where they did them, and what materials they used, I was able to picture in some detail what different kinds of Dakota camps would have looked like. Housing, other buildings, food-storage facilities, work areas, and associated tools and implements would make fall ricing camps, late-winter maple sugaring camps, deer hunting camps, and wintering camps look different when inhabited and different when archaeological sites.

My research showed that the encampment at Little Rapids conformed to what one would expect to find at sites I called "summer logistical bases," a term chosen following archaeologist Lewis Binford's article about sites used by hunters and foragers (Binford 1980, 5). Binford's "new archaeology" of the late 1960s and early 1970s is notable for its insistence on scientific methods and its heavy use of archaeological jargon. The pretentiousness of the term "summer logistical base" embarrasses me now, especially after discovering the more meaningful phrase used by nineteenth-century Dakota elders. They referred to Inyan Ceyaka Atonwan as their "summer planting village" (Riggs 1893, 158, 180).

My research also reinforced the value of examining women's and men's activity patterns. Just as the earlier task analysis of four Indian groups had helped break down simplistic notions about sex-based divisions of labor, the application of the approach to Little Rapids undermined the common tendency among archaeologists to generalize from one site to the whole culture.

Still, my thinking and writing about Little Rapids frustrated me. I was increasingly haunted by a criticism that Indians frequently express: that archaeologists and anthropologists exploit Indian sites and materials in order to build their own careers (McNickle 1972; Medicine, Ortiz, and McNickle 1972). I worried about using Little Rapids to make a series of points to other archaeologists that Indian people would find trivial, offensive, or both. By 1984, when I completed the final draft of my paper about the type of site represented at Little Rapids, my uneasiness about the dissonance between my feminist insights and the archaeology I continued to practice had intensified.

Those of us who produce knowledge about other people hold a powerful and privileged position. Male domination of the field of anthropology has produced distortions about women in many cultural settings and time periods. Similarly, Indian people have had little part in producing archaeological knowledge about their past, and archaeologists have surely produced and perpetuated similar distortions about Indian histories and cultures. I did not want to do this. I no longer wanted to investigate the archaeology of Indian people unless their perspectives and voices were incorporated into the work.

For some time I was stuck. How could a non-Indian person do Indian-centered work? When men ask me if they can do feminist work, I say yes. Although not all feminists agree, I do not think a person has to be female to detect gender bias or to write from a feminist perspective. I wondered if this same principle were true for non-Indian people doing Indian studies.

It was time for me to talk to Dakota people. In 1985 a Minnesota Historical Society staff member introduced me to Chris Cavender. My initial conversation with him was awkward. It seemed late to be consulting with Dakota people on a project designed several years earlier without their involvement. Cavender had not heard of the Little Rapids site, and although he was cordial, he seemed distant and, maybe, suspicious. Candid about his impressions of "anthros," as he called us, he openly expressed skepticism about the motives of most academic researchers.

During our meeting I mentioned that written records referred to a man named Mazomani as a prominent leader at Little Rapids during the early decades of the 1800s. Chris[4] said nothing at the time, but he telephoned me later to ask if we could visit the site together.

---

4. In this book I often refer to participants in the Little Rapids project by their first names. This reflects the informal though respectful character of our work relationships.

Mazomani, it turned out, was related to him through his mother, Elsie M. Cavender.

During the next few months we made several trips to the site, sometimes bringing family members related to Mazomani and Chris. These visits were emotionally moving. Finally, I was meeting and talking to Dakota people at a location that was theirs by kinship. They were glad to be there, and we shared an appreciation for this historic place that, unlike many Indian sites, had been shielded from construction and other destructive land uses. Although livestock had grazed at Little Rapids after the Dakota left in the 1850s, the earth had never been plowed because bedrock lay too close to the ground surface. Between 1968 and 1970, Northern States Power Company had purchased land parcels along the Minnesota River that included the site but never developed it. Finally, in 1979, the area became part of the Carver Rapids Wayside within the Minnesota Valley National Wildlife Refuge (USFWS 1982, 3–2).

Over the years major damage had been done by artifact collectors and by "amateurs," people who practice archaeology as a hobby. Drawn there by the burial mounds at the southern end of the site, they had been digging at Little Rapids for decades, and signs of their activity scarred the landscape. It was excruciating for me to walk with Dakota people near the disturbed mounds and witness the extent of some amateurs' disrespect. Digging in burial mounds on state or private lands had been prohibited by amendments to the state's Private Cemeteries Act (MN ST 307.08) in 1978, 1980, and 1986, adopted with the support of Minnesota's professional archaeologists.[5] Little Rapids, however, was not easily protected from looting because of its remote location.

As the 1985–86 school year began, Chris and I developed plans to teach together at Little Rapids. Then we secured some university funding and recruited other instructors. Carolynn ("Carrie") I. Schommer, a Dakota-language instructor at the university who is also a descendant of Mazomani, taught crew members the Dakota language. Edward J. Cushing, a university ecologist, did field studies with students

5. At the federal level, the Archaeological Resources Protection Act (93 Stat. 721) of 1979 requires a permit to dig in burial mounds on federal land. The Native American Graves Protection and Repatriation Act (104 Stat. 3048) of 1990 provides more guidelines and protections for burial mounds on state and private as well as federal lands.

about the natural history and environment of the area. He, Chris, and Carrie worked together comparing Dakota, English, and Latin names for plants near Little Rapids that were—and still are—important to Dakota people. Sara M. Evans, a women's history professor at the university, helped us critically evaluate nineteenth-century documentary records and place them in their Euro-American cultural context. Chris shared what he knew from Dakota sources about some of the people and events described in those documents. Things were not always simple. In June 1986, after a four-year hiatus in our digging at Little Rapids, a dramatic thunderstorm struck the area on Saturday night before the field school was to begin. All access roads were flooded, and for more than a week we had to ferry eighteen people to and from the site daily. An inauspicious start. Chris and Carrie later told me they thought the thunderstorm might be a warning about the project and that they had almost abandoned it. This was just one of many storms that summer.

In addition, I worried that crew members or non-Dakota visitors might make insensitive or racist remarks that would stir up political or interpersonal storms. This happened occasionally, but we worked our way through these episodes.

For the first time in my archaeological career, a project felt right. We worked as an interdisciplinary, multicultural team. Descendants of the people who had lived at the site were there, speaking Dakota, telling us about Dakota culture, and helping us understand more about the small clues to their past that we found buried just beneath the surface. Every day Chris and Carrie talked with us about Dakota family and community life, Dakota place-names and words for the seasons and months of the year, the Dakota council fires, and Dakota spirituality (Cavender 1986). Before we dug into the earth, Chris spoke briefly in Dakota, expressing our collective respect for the spirit of the place and his hope that as the project's leader I would be guided by sensitivity and wisdom.

When Amos Owen, a Dakota elder and spiritual leader, conducted a pipe ceremony shortly after our field season began, he communicated in words that had been spoken there for centuries until Dakota voices were silenced at Little Rapids in the 1850s. Chris, Carrie, and I had hoped that Amos could visit the site earlier, before we began to dig. To us the pipe ceremony symbolized the Dakota people's permission to work there, as important as the authorizations already secured from

FIG. 2. Elsie Cavender speaking to Randy Withrow and other students at her home, 1986

the state archaeologist and the state's natural resources department. After the ceremony, Amos spoke to us about his own spiritual development and Dakota beliefs. He thoroughly tempered his remarks with wisdom and humor. Just after his departure, a tremendous thunderstorm struck.

Many other memorable events marked that summer. Because Chris and Carrie were there, Indian people frequently visited the site. One day a group of young people from Minneapolis arrived, and Indian children again ran and laughed at Little Rapids. Many asked permission from the spirits when they picked ripe berries to eat. On another occasion we visited Elsie Cavender and members of her family at the Upper Sioux Community near Granite Falls (FIG. 2). After preparing a feast for us, she told us her family's account of the 1862 war between Dakota people and new settlers in which Mazomani had been killed. Her story, so quietly and gently told, was painful to hear. Later Carrie took us to Mazomani's grave on a high ridge above the Minnesota River.

We learned a great deal from the Dakota people who worked with us. Although they showed some interest in how we worked and the things we found, they were most attracted to the place, especially to the burial mounds whose presence permeates the physical and spiritual landscape at Little Rapids.

I BEGAN WRITING this book about Little Rapids with several goals in mind. First, I wanted to communicate in an easily accessible way what we had learned about the Wahpeton community during a turbulent period of its history. Second, I wanted to highlight women's activities and the relations between men and women, topics typically ignored in archaeological writings. Third, I wanted to incorporate Dakota voices, visions, and perspectives into the story.

Initially, I returned to my earlier analysis of Dakota men's and women's activities, hoping to expand that study. I started with two sets of data: information and artifacts from the Little Rapids site, now mapped, sorted, identified, and counted; and documentary evidence from nineteenth-century written accounts, organized into tables with titles such as "Gender-Specific Task Inventory: Women/Men," "Task Seasonality," "Task Materials: Women/Men," and "Men's and Women's Material Inventory." Although Euro-American men wrote most of the nineteenth-century descriptions of Dakota life, several women also left eyewitness accounts. In addition, Charles A. Eastman (Ohiyesa), a Wahpeton man, recorded experiences from his childhood in the mid-1800s (C. Eastman [1902] 1971). These remarkably consistent sources often included detailed descriptions of men's and women's work and activities. During the digging we had recovered evidence of numerous resource-procurement, processing, and storage activities; signs of clothing, tool, ornament, and ammunition manufacturing; and traces of housing. Through close analysis of the tasks as described in the literature, I hoped we could link elements of the Little Rapids archaeological assemblage to the men, women, and children who lived in the community.

Yet as I pursued this approach and, at the same time, reflected on my recent experiences with Dakota people at the site, I became dissatisfied. I found the task-differentiation approach too constraining as a way of writing about what life was like for the nineteenth-century people. Like other taxonomic schemes, it generated distanced and lifeless representations of the past. This was not how I wanted to portray the Wahpeton people who had lived at the site when Euro-Americans began moving into the territory. So, finally, I put aside my tables enumerating activities, schedules, spaces, and tools and began to experiment with a new way of presenting the past.

I turned my attention to an artifact that we had discovered in 1980 in a garbage dump. It was a small antler awl handle, about three inches long and delicately inscribed with a series of dots and lines. The handle would have held a short, pointed iron tip of about the same length, making a tool for perforating leather and other materials. I felt certain that a Wahpeton woman had once used the tool at Little Rapids and that its inscriptions conveyed a great deal about her accomplishments to those who understood their meaning. The awl handle became an important symbol to me.

In response to this evocative find, I wrote the story of how the awl might have been used and lost. In many ways, that work represents the culmination of what I have learned between the time of my visits to the mounds in Madison with my grandfather and my visits to the mounds at Little Rapids with members of Mazomani's family. Through this account I hope to give readers a sense of Dakota culture in those times and to stimulate curiosity about the site and the people who left no written records of themselves.

The chapters that follow the story unravel it. They incorporate voices and viewpoints other than my own—those of the Dakota people, as well as the fur traders, officials, explorers, and missionaries that the Indians encountered, sometimes in harmony but more often in conflict. Throughout I have tried to convey the turmoil of the times and to avoid the rhetoric of archaeology that frequently obscures the people being studied.

Shaping my work are the ongoing tensions between archaeologists and Indian people. These conflicts exemplify the archaeological premise that the past shapes the present. A viewpoint archaeologists less often acknowledge is that the present shapes our rendering of the past.

T W O

WHAT
THIS
AWL
MEANS

THE WOMEN AND CHILDREN of Inyan Ceyaka Atonwan (Little Rapids) had been working at the maple sugar camps since Istawicayazan wi (the Moon of Sore Eyes, or March). At the same time, most of the men had been far from the village trapping muskrats. When Wozupi wi (the Moon for Planting, or May) came, fifteen households eagerly reunited in their bark lodges (FIG. 3) near the river. Hard work lay ahead; they needed to replenish their stores of food and other supplies consumed over the long winter.

In the first days after their return, the women repaired the houses they would be living in for the next few months. They reinforced or replaced the basswood-bark lashing holding the wood pole framework together. Then they reset the wall posts, roof rafters, and sections of the elm bark walls and roof that harsh winter winds, ice, and snow had dislodged. Several of the older lodges had been damaged beyond repair, so the women cleared and leveled the ground with their hoes to prepare for new dwellings. Soon everyone in the community moved from their portable, skin-covered tipis, which they used during the winter months and while traveling, into the cooler summer lodges.

Most of the men and boys spread out from the village daily to fish or hunt ducks, turtles, and small game. Meanwhile, groups of women and girls collected firewood and building supplies and gathered

FIG. 3. *Indian Village on the Mississippi near Fort Snelling,* watercolor
by Seth Eastman, 1840s

the late spring vegetables and fruits beginning to appear in the surrounding woods, prairies, and marshes. Every day they watched for
the appearance of strawberries. When the fruit ripened, the women
knew it was time to soak their seed corn. After the kernels sprouted,
they planted it in the rich soil near the slough where wild artichokes
grew.

One day some villagers brought their tanned furs and maple sugar
to the lodge of Jean Baptiste Faribault. He lived among them a few
months each year with his Dakota wife, Pelagie. In exchange for furs
and maple sugar, Faribault gave them glass beads, silver ornaments,
tin kettles, and iron knives, awl tips, axes, hatchets, and hoes for their
summer work. On this day Faribault seemed uneasy; he told them
that a "praying man" named Stephen R. Riggs planned to visit them
soon.

Mazomani (Iron Walker), a prominent man in the Village at the
Rapids community, was among the Dakota visiting the trading post
that day. Faribault respected Mazomani as a leader of the Wakan Wacipi
(medicine dance lodge), and Faribault knew that Mazomani had recently announced a dance to be held on the day that Riggs was now

FIG. 4. *Indians in Council,* watercolor by Seth Eastman, 1850

expected. Faribault also knew that missionaries such as Riggs viewed the Wakan Wacipi with contempt, finding its practices imposing and absurd. Hoping to prevent a conflict between Riggs and Mazomani, Faribault suggested delaying the dance, to which the people, after some deliberation, agreed.

When Riggs visited Little Rapids, he did not stay long. Speaking Dakota as well as he could, he asked to talk to the "chief men" (FIG. 4). Mazomani and several others came forward, curious to know what he wanted. Riggs offered to teach the men how to farm, apparently not knowing that Dakota women would never willingly give up their cornfields. His ideas about proper men's and women's work amused them, but his suggestion that they injure the earth by cutting it with a plow seemed incomprehensible. When he next asked to establish a mission at Little Rapids and suggested that he replace Mazomani as the community's spiritual leader, they were insulted and angry. Abruptly, they told Riggs to leave. So after only a half-day at Little

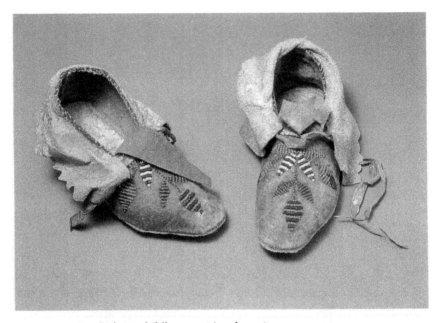

FIG. 5. Dakota child's moccasins, late 1800s

Rapids, he and his party continued up the Minnesota River, looking for another location for a mission and not comprehending why the people refused his offers. The next day, Mazomani announced that the medicine dance would be held during Wasuton wi (the Moon when Corn Is Gathered, or August), and the community resumed its summer work without further intrusion.

Mazomani and Hazawin (Blueberry Woman) were proud of their daughter, Mazaokiyewin (Woman Who Talks to Iron). The day after visiting Faribault, they had given her some glass beads and a new iron awl tip. The tip was the right size to fit into the small antler handle that Hazawin had given Mazaokiyewin when she went to dwell alone at the time of her first menses. Mazaokiyewin used the sharp-pointed awl for punching holes in pieces of leather before stitching them together with deer sinew. Though young, she had already established a reputation among the people at Inyan Ceyaka Atonwan for creativity and excellence in quillwork and beadwork.

Mazaokiyewin's mother and grandmothers had taught her to keep a careful record of her accomplishments, so whenever she finished quilling or beading moccasins (FIG. 5), she remembered to impress a small dot on the fine awl handle that Hazawin had made for her. When

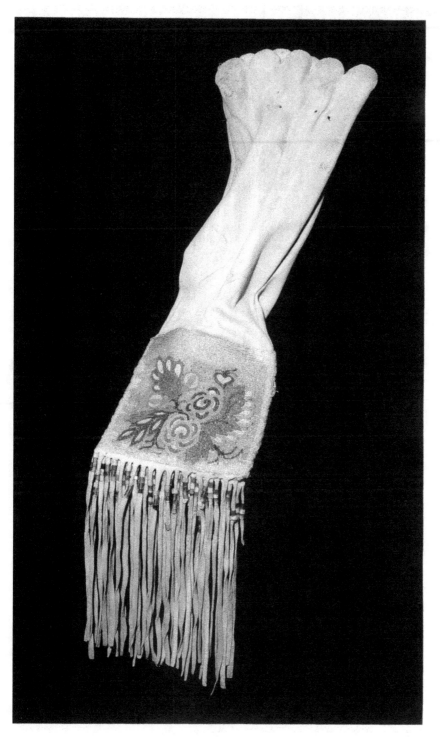

FIG. 6. Dakota beaded pipe bag, about 1850

FIG. 7.
Awl handle showing diamond-
shaped pattern

FIG. 8.
Awl handle showing
red-dot detail

FIG. 9. *Medicine Dance of the Sioux or Dakota Indians on the St.Peters River—near Fort Snelling,* watercolor by Seth Eastman, 1847

Mazaokiyewin completed more complicated work, such as sewing and decorating a buckskin dress or pipe bag (FIG. 6), she formed diamond-shaped clusters of four small dots which symbolized the powers of the four directions that influenced her life in many ways (FIG. 7). She liked to expose the handle of this small tool as she carried it in its beaded case so that others could see she was doing her best to ensure the well-being of their community.

When she engraved the dots into her awl handle, she carefully marked each one with red pigment, made by boiling sumac berries with a small root found in the ground near the village (FIG. 8). Dakota people associated the color red with women and their life forces. Red also represented the east, where the sun rose to give knowledge, wisdom, and understanding. Red symbolized Mazaokiyewin's aspirations to these qualities.

When the designated day in Wasuton wi arrived, Mazomani led the people in the medicine dance near the burial place of their ancestors (FIG. 9). Members of the medicine lodge danced within an enclosed oval area, separated from the audience by a low, hide-covered fence.

FIG. 10. *Guarding the Corn Fields,* watercolor by Seth Eastman, early 1850s

To guarantee the success of the event, dancers wore necklaces of carved bone beads, cowrie shells, and brass thimbles holding dried fireflies. After the dancing everyone feasted on the finest of foods, prepared for this occasion over fires at one end of the dance enclosure.

One hot day following the dance, Mazaokiyewin gathered together all of the leatherwork she had finished since returning to Inyan Ceyaka Atonwan after the spring hunting and sugaring seasons. The women had already finished making new clothes, bags, moccasins, and tools in preparation for the fall deer hunt. They had also completed harvesting their corn (FIG. 10), which was dried and stored underground in large bark baskets near their lodges for use in winter when fresh vegetables were not available. Now, Mazaokiyewin eagerly anticipated the quilling contest and feast called by a woman of a neighboring household to honor a family member. Mazaokiyewin knew she had produced more beaded and quilled articles than most of the community's young women, and she looked forward to bringing recognition to her parents and grandparents.

The lodge where the contest was held grew hot during the day as each woman spread out the items she had made for others to view.

The women stayed inside to avoid the intense heat and sun, but as a thunderstorm approached, the lodge grew stifling. An elder asked Mazaokiyewin to bring more drinking water. Mazaokiyewin ran down the slope from the village to the spring near the slough, glad to be close to the cool water. She thought of taking a quick swim, but the thunder sounded closer, and it started to rain—lightly at first, then, as it often did on hot summer days, falling in great sheets across the village.

She started uphill carrying the *miniapahtapi* (skin water bags) carefully, but near the quilling-contest lodge she slipped on the muddy path where water had pooled in the driving rain. As she struggled to regain her footing without dropping the bags, the leather strap holding her awl in its case broke (FIG. 11), and the small awl dropped to the ground. It fell close to one of the cooking fires outside the lodge entrance.

Mazaokiyewin did not miss her awl that day, because as soon as she entered the lodge with the water, the host of the contest took her hand and escorted her to the center of the crowd. The host had already counted each woman's pieces and distributed a stick for each. Mazaokiyewin had accumulated more sticks than all but three older women. The host then led the four to the place of honor in the lodge and gave them their food first to honor their accomplishments. Later, the results of this contest would be recorded for all to see on the hides lining the walls of the lodge. This pleased Hazawin and Mazomani.

The heavy rain that day had scattered debris over the village, and on the day after the quilling contest and medicine dance, people joined together to clean up the encampment. Using old hides and baskets, they carried off loads of fallen branches, wet fire ash and charcoal, and the remains of the feast to the community dump above the slough. Somehow, Mazaokiyewin's small awl was swept up and carried off with other garbage from the quilling contest. It disappeared in the dump as the villagers emptied one basketload after another on top of it.

Later, the loss of the awl saddened Mazaokiyewin and Hazawin, but they knew the handle was nearly worn out, and both realized it was more a girl's tool than a woman's. Mazaokiyewin was almost a woman ready to establish her own household, no longer a child of her mother's lodge. It was time to put aside her girl-tools, she knew, but she had intended to keep this awl. Its finely incised dots and

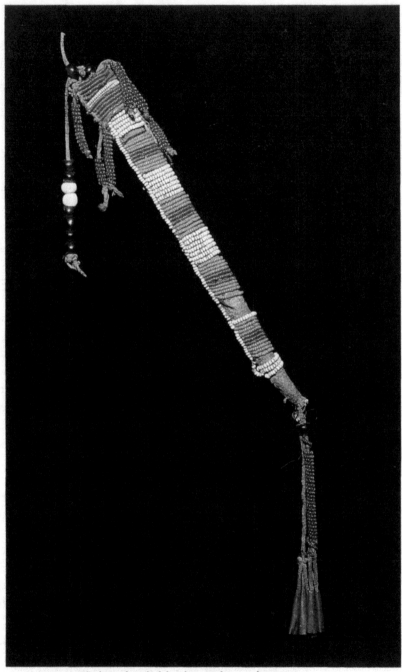

FIG. 11. Dakota beaded leather awl case, late 1800s

engraved lines showed how well she had learned adult tasks, and she took as much pleasure in displaying it as her mother did in watching others admire it.

One evening, as Mazaokiyewin and Hazawin stored the last of the summer's harvested corn, they were reminded of "praying-man" Riggs and his strange belief that men should plant corn. They had heard rumors all summer that more *wasicun* (white men) were coming up the river, and as they prepared to leave the planting village for fall ricing and hunting camps, they took special care to camouflage the areas where they hid their winter food supplies.

The following day, they packed the equipment that the family would need over the next several months. As they assembled their hide-working tools, they spoke again of Mazaokiyewin's missing awl. They realized that their feeling of loss was not simply about that one small tool. Instead, as fall approached and they prepared to leave Inyan Ceyaka Atonwan, they had troubling premonitions about the future.

THREE

OTHER
AWL
STORIES

ARCHAEOLOGISTS TYPICALLY IGNORE biography. The names of people who lived at most sites are inaccessible, unrecorded, and usually long forgotten. Although the materials that archaeologists uncover reflect the unique individuals who created and used them, archaeological descriptions and interpretations tend to be impersonal, even when the site's inhabitants are known from written records. Similarly, archaeologists seldom write about themselves, their interests, their perspectives, or their feelings about practicing archaeology. Not surprisingly, their writings tend to be lifeless, with little sense of individual character, action, motivation, or emotion.

The way that archaeologists have treated awls from the fur trade era exemplifies these tendencies. Prior to contact with Euro-American traders, Indian people fashioned perforating tools from a variety of materials such as needle-sharp fish bones or sharpened deer bones. Fur traders added metal nails, spikes, and more specialized awl tips to this inventory. Sometimes Indians hafted these tips into handles fashioned from antler or bone.

In reports about two sites that are historically documented—Fort Michilimackinac in Michigan and Rock Island in Wisconsin—archaeologists Lyle M. Stone and Ronald J. Mason described trade awls similar to those found at Little Rapids. Had I followed their writing style, I might have classified and discussed awls along with other, presumably related, artifact types under a heading such as "Household

Context of Utilization—Maintenance and Repair" (Stone 1974, 155–62). My emphasis would have been on the metal awl tips, not the awl handles, and my description might have read like this:

> A total of four metal awls (FIG. 12) were found during excavations at Little Rapids. These have been classified on the basis of four attributes: (1) means of attachment of awl tip to handle, (2) cross-section shape, (3) size as defined by dimension of length, and (4) material of manufacture. All four are made of iron, with "offset attachments" conforming most closely to what Stone has identified as Type 1, Variety a.

Then, in a section called "Discussion," I might quote Stone directly and note: "Although awls have been reported from several other sites, . . . this limited evidence does not permit cross dating. The . . . quantity and . . . spatial distribution of awls indicate that they were commonly used . . . throughout the period of site occupation. . . . Trade-goods lists indicate that awls were an important trade item with the Indians" (Stone 1974, 159). End of discussion.

Stone did not write about the bone or antler awl handles shown in a photograph with the metal awl tips, although like the tips, the handles also varied in size, shape, and form (Stone 1974, 156). Mason also approached awls taxonomically, describing the metal tips in tables titled "European Trade Goods" and "Aboriginal Artifacts Made from Trade Materials" (Mason 1986, 61). He discussed neither tips nor handles, although his report included a photograph of an iron tip hafted into a plain bone handle. In comments about this photograph, Mason remarked that "it appears that bone and antler tool making survived longer in the native repertoire than pottery making and common flint knapping" (Mason 1986, 53).

The style of presentation favored by Stone and Mason channels our attention as readers in specific but unacknowledged ways. Their descriptions inadvertently convey negative messages about Indian people and culture, despite the neutral, objective-sounding language. For example, an important but hidden assumption in their works is that European-produced metal awl tips are more important than Indian-produced awl handles. Built into Stone's and Mason's classifications and table titles, this theme leads to emphasis on metal awl tips as markers of European influence on Indians and implies the disintegration of

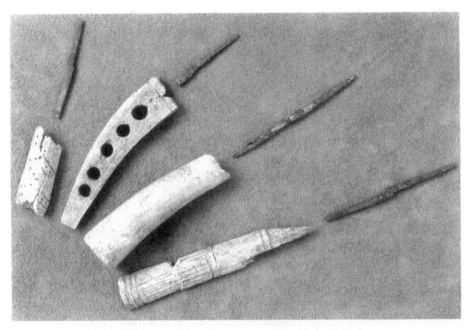

FIG. 12. Awl tips and handles excavated at Little Rapids

native culture. This would have been insulting, annoying, or simply wrong to Indians who used awls, particularly to women who inscribed their bone or antler handles to display publicly their accomplishments. To them the metal tips might have been simply a convenient addition to their hide-working tool kits, not a sign of cultural weakness or decline.

Complicating the problem, Stone and Mason used artifact classification systems designed for analyzing European, not Indian, material goods. Stone's category, "Household Context of Utilization," includes awls used by Indians as well as artifacts used by French and British residents of Fort Michilimackinac. Awls and other sewing equipment fall into the narrow tool subclassification, "Maintenance and repair." While seemingly neutral, this classification suggests that awls were merely "support" tools for maintaining or repairing other more useful or important objects. Furthermore, Stone placed awls within a household, or domestic, female-associated sphere, rather than in an implied public, male-associated sphere. He visually represented this gendered association with an introductory chapter illustration depicting two eighteenth-century French women doing embroidery (Stone 1974, 155).

The powerful idea that a domestic-public dichotomy characterizes all human societies prevails in Western thought. Social life is conceptually divided into two differentially valued parts that are gendered. The domestic, female sphere is less important than the male-dominated public domain. In recent decades feminist anthropologists have shown this to be an arbitrary division derived from nineteenth-century European social theory and one that does not accurately describe community life for many groups in the past or present (Rosaldo 1980; H. Moore 1988, 21–25). Artifact taxonomies such as Stone's, with its implied subdivisions by gender, inadvertently relegate women, their activities, and their tools to a secondary role in society. When applied to awls, the dichotomy leads us away from, rather than toward, insights about the original meaning or use of these artifacts.

These descriptions of awls communicate other unacknowledged messages. Like many archaeologists, Stone and Mason rarely mentioned people or their activities directly. They conveyed no real sense of people making, trading for, displaying, or working with awls. As a result, the awls lack context, associations, and meaning, except insofar as they measure the passage of time or the influence of whites on Indians. Although the archaeologists' writing style is intentionally depersonalized and object centered, it still conveys feelings. Boring, tedious, and confusing-to-read descriptions of awls affect readers, who inevitably transfer their feelings to the people who once made or used the tools.

As an archaeologist I can ignore the written text and tables and simply look at the pictures, comparing what I found at "my" site with what they found at "their" site. But why would most readers bother with the tables, charts, and tool descriptions that actively discourage, rather than encourage, learning about groups of people in the past? Why do archaeologists write dense technical reports in esoteric language instead of lively cultural studies?

Reviewing trends in written archaeology from the eighteenth century to the present, archaeologist Ian Hodder similarly observed that contemporary archaeological reports are "at best . . . dull, excessively long, detailed and expensive and read by no one except the delirious specialist." He continued, "It often seems to me as if the code has become everything, pursued for its own sake. The public value of the lists and dry descriptions is questionable" (Hodder 1989, 273).

Although archaeologists have paid little critical attention to the political implications of their writing styles, the rhetoric of cultural anthropology has recently been subjected to a good deal of scrutiny, debate, and experimentation (Clifford and Marcus 1986; Rosaldo 1989; Mascia-Lees et al. 1989). In February 1986, in the midst of planning the summer field program at Little Rapids with Chris Cavender, I heard Stanford University anthropologist Renato Rosaldo talk about writing ethnography (descriptions of cultures). He eloquently demonstrated how the dominant, legitimate form of ethnographic writing, a "detached, dehumanizing, descriptive idiom," can undermine "the anthropological project of understanding other cultures." He also argued that the authority of this kind of discourse "has become so well established, so much taken for granted, that it appears within the norms of the discipline, not as one rhetorical mode of representation among others, but as the one and only legitimate form for telling the literal truth about other people's lifeways. Yet no single rhetoric, whatever current fashions may dictate, has a monopoly on objectivity" (Rosaldo 1986, 14–15, 32).

Rosaldo then asked us to apply descriptions written in that mode to our own culture. This simple turnabout showed how easily everyday experiences can be caricatured or misrepresented through so-called objective writing. "Allowing forms of writing that have been marginalized or banned altogether to gain legitimacy," Rosaldo suggested as an alternative, would "enable the discipline to approximate people's lives from a number of angles of vision" and apprehend "the range of human possibilities in their fullest complexity" (Rosaldo 1986, 33).

Rosaldo's call for writing anthropology in new and varied ways became especially relevant to me as I tried to convey the meanings of the inscribed awl handle from Little Rapids. The conventional archaeological style of describing awls seemed singularly inappropriate for this particular tool.

INSCRIBE: "TO FIX or impress deeply or lastingly in the mind, memory . . . " (*Webster's New World Dictionary*, 2nd ed.).

August 11, 1980, was cool and cloudy, an unusual day in what was otherwise an extremely hot, dry summer. We had recently begun the second session of our first summer field-school program at Little Rapids, offered for students with weekday jobs.

It had rained during the night, and the crew members spent a good portion of the morning cleaning up debris scattered over our excavations. One group was working in a section I had named "Activity Area II" and tentatively identified as a dump—or midden, in archaeological language. I had based this preliminary interpretation on the very distinctive deposits of fire ash, small clusters of fish bones, broken animal bones, turtle shells, charcoal, nuts, and berry seeds distributed over the area at every level from just below the present-day ground surface to a depth of fifty centimeters. We had excavated a number of two-meter squares in this area during the first weeks of the summer, so the cleaning up process required time and patience.

The dump area was roughly oval shaped, more than eight meters long by three meters wide. Mixed in with things intentionally left there were broken tools and small ornaments undoubtedly lost rather than discarded: a small penknife, a brooch and earring made from rolled silver, a cut-iron projectile point—things people must have eventually missed but never found.

Discovering so many remnants of daily life in one small area always evokes images. We easily imagined people cleaning fish, butchering animals, processing plants, cooking meals, removing wet ash from fire pits, sweeping out lodges, clearing away remains from feasts, and, finally, carrying basket loads of this refuse to a community dump. The residents may have brought garbage to the high ground above the slough to keep their lodges or work areas free from decaying organic matter that would attract rodents and other pests. For whatever reason they disposed of their waste there, they unknowingly formed a part of the site that revealed much about their way of life.

It was in the corner of a two-meter-square excavation in the dump, twenty centimeters below the ground surface, that we found the inscribed awl handle that day. "A beautiful, carved bone handle, red paint visible on one side," I recorded in my field notes after photographing it where it rested (FIG. 13). Joan Junquiera, the student excavator who discovered it, wrote in her daily notes that she was "overjoyed" by her "great discovery!" Her digging partner, Mary Ellen Kelly, was less enthusiastic about her day's finds: "Well, we didn't have to stop for artifacts. . . . Held it down to some lead, a metal awl [tip],

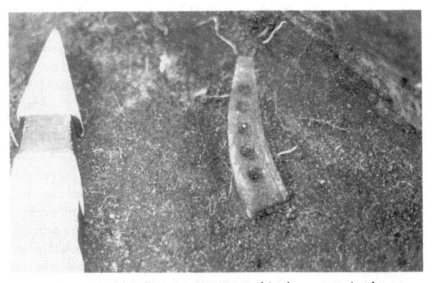

FIG. 13. Awl handle as it was uncovered in the community dump

and a long . . . bead." None of us realized then the connection between the handle Joan had uncovered and the awl tip Mary Ellen had
found nearby.

From the beginning, there was something remarkable about the
decorated handle. Although buried in the dump for years, it was un-
broken and well preserved, still showing traces of the red pigment marking rows of dots decorating the edges of the tool. Surely it had been
lost, not thrown away.

When I examined the handle more closely, I felt increasingly intrigued by the person who made it. I assumed it was a woman, since
women were responsible for working hides among the Dakota. She
had drilled five holes down the length of the handle and etched
patterns of dots and lines over all its surfaces. She might have used
the small, sharpened nails or fragments of window glass we found in
the midden to etch her inscriptions.

Along one edge of the handle, she had impressed a row of fourteen equally spaced dots, marking each with a dab of red pigment.
One dot was scratched over with an "x" as if she had miscounted or
for some other reason wanted to erase it. On the opposite edge of
the handle, another set of impressed red dots formed a different motif:
six dots in a row followed by diamond-shaped clusters of four red dots

each. Inscribed lines and dots covered the handle, surely signifying something to the person who crafted it and to others in the community who viewed it.

For some time, the meaning of the marks eluded me, and the inscriptions remained undecipherable. None of the archaeological sources I consulted mentioned such markings. I knew only that the awl handle was unusual and that someone intended it to look the way it did. Furthermore, the discovery of another inscribed bone handle at the site, a small fragment with a different etched design of lines and dots, suggested that the awl handle was not an idiosyncratic or one-of-a-kind find (see FIG. 12).

Some time later, a student, Sarah J. Oliver, brought me a book in which she had marked a passage that explained the meaning of the awl inscriptions. Although the author, historian Royal B. Hassrick, described Lakota or Western Sioux people from 1830 to 1870, the descriptions could also apply to the Eastern Dakota, who are linguistically and culturally related to the Lakota.

Hassrick provided a wealth of detailed information about women's work and values that he learned from a Lakota woman, Blue Whirlwind. She may well have been the source that told him:

> In the same way that men kept war records, so did women keep count of their accomplishments. Ambition to excel was real among females. Accomplishments were recorded by means of dots incised along the handles of the polished elkhorn scraping tools. The dots on one side were black, on the other red. Each black dot represented a tanned robe; each red dot represented ten hides or one tipi. When a woman had completed one hundred robes or ten tipis, she was privileged to place an incised circle at the base of the handle of her scraper (Hassrick 1964, xiii, 42).

Finally the inscriptions on the awl handle became meaningful.

Sisseton-Wahpeton historian Elijah Black Thunder reported that Sisseton and Wahpeton Dakota women inscribed their horn- and wood-handled scrapers to record the number of hides and tipis they had worked (Black Thunder et al. 1975, 106). Anthropologist Alanson B. Skinner reported the same for Sisseton women (Skinner 1919, 167). No written sources from the nineteenth century say specifically that Wahpeton women marked awl handles in a similar way, but evidence from the Little Rapids site provides tangible evidence that they did.

This interpretation is consistent with other information Hassrick presented about the importance of women's awls. He was told, again probably by Blue Whirlwind, that when a girl experienced her first menses, "she notified her mother, who took her to a separate wigwam or small tipi. Sequestered there for four days, the mother would ceremoniously teach her the art of quill embroidery and moccasin-making. As one old person expressed it, 'Even though she has learned quilling before, the girl must quill continuously for four days. If she does this she will be good with the awl; if she does not, she will never be industrious'" (Hassrick 1964, 41–42).

Hassrick also described public events where nineteenth-century Lakota women exhibited their work.

Rattling Blanket Woman went from guest to guest and after asking what they had made, gave each a stick for every piece of work. When everyone had received the sticks to which they were entitled, the hostess took by the hand the woman who had the fourth most sticks and led her to a place of honor. She then escorted the woman who had the third most and seated her in front of the first woman chosen, and so on until the winner was placed before all as became her position.

When the women agreed that the one chosen was the rightful winner, others brought food, serving first the four winners in the order of their industry, then passing food to the others. To record the event, marks were placed on the dew cloth or tipi lining of the Red Council Lodge [*where tribal leaders met*]. Small marks were made to represent the work done prior to puberty, larger marks for later work, and over them was the maker's name. Thus Rattling Blanket Woman's ten small marks and four large ones were designated by the drawing of a rattle superimposed upon a blanket with a line extending from it to the marks. This was her "quilling count," and just as a man displayed his war honors in the Red Council Lodge, so a woman displayed her abilities (Hassrick 1964, 43).

For me, discovering the meaning of the awl inscriptions was like cracking a code or being able to read some ancient, previously undeciphered text for the first time. I began looking at artifacts in a fresh way, my imagination untethered from the constraints of traditional archaeology's writing conventions and taxonomic devices. The awl handle could be removed from the "Household Context of Utilization—Maintenance and Repair" category, liberating me, as well as the woman whose work and accomplishments it marked. The awl inscriptions provided a kind of access to the people at Little Rapids that I had never before imagined possible.

FIG. 14. Minnesota River at Inyan Ceyaka Atonwan, or Little Rapids

FOUR

CULTURES
IN
CONFLICT

O VER THE CENTURIES Little Rapids has drawn to it many different peoples (FIG. 14). Strategically situated and rich in natural resources, it sits atop a bedrock plateau on the east side of the Minnesota River— an island of high ground more than a mile square surrounded by marshes, swamps, and lowland forests. Melting glacial ice formed the physical character of this place more than nine thousand years ago as a river outlet drained Glacial Lake Agassiz and in the process carved the Minnesota River valley into the landscape. The present river, a small stream compared with the great one that created the valley, slowly meanders across the broad floodplain, curving around knobs of bedrock such as the one at Little Rapids on its way to Fort Snelling and the Mississippi River. At a bend in the river near the site, water flowing over rock creates two sets of small rapids, the only ones found along the entire course of the river and a landmark recognized by Indians and non-Indians in their names for this place.

Forty feet below the site and separating it from the rapids is a small, marshy basin and floodplain forest known as Johnson's Slough, a permanent scar left behind as a reminder of the shifting river channel (Withrow 1986b). The rich array of plant, animal, and mineral resources near the rapids has attracted many inhabitants over time (Cushing 1986; Stolen 1988; USFWS 1982). Most of the Wahpeton activities we eventually discovered archaeologically took place in these marshes, forests, and grasslands, but Wahpetons were not the first people to use the site.

The earliest residents, probably distant relatives of the nineteenth-century Dakota, inhabited Little Rapids long before Europeans came to North America. We saw remnants of their presence during our excavations, mostly locally made pottery and stone tools. These peoples probably also built the site's earthen burial mounds. Although these constructions have never been analyzed or dated, they resemble other mounds in the midwestern United States built by Indians to bury deceased community members, a tradition that continued after contact with Europeans. Archaeologists have noted that Dakota villages in Minnesota often have mounds nearby, silent testimony of the deep connections to place among the Dakota (Anfinson 1984).

Written sources refer to the presence of a Wahpeton Dakota community at Little Rapids by the turn of the nineteenth century, although Dakota peoples had probably lived there many centuries before any outsider recorded their presence. By 1800 the Wahpeton would have shared their territories with a succession of fur traders who established seasonal posts near the river.

The story of Mazaokiyewin's lost awl in chapter 2 introduces seven people connected to the community in the 1830s to 1840s. Mazomani, fur trader Jean B. Faribault, and Faribault's Dakota wife Pelagie Hanse lived there or nearby, according to written sources. Cavender family history identifies Mazaokiyewin as the daughter of Mazomani and Hazawin, although no surviving records specifically document either woman's presence at Little Rapids. Missionary Stephen Riggs and his wife Mary reported stopping there in the summer of 1843.

In 1851, through the Treaty of Traverse des Sioux, the U.S. government formally acquired the land around Little Rapids. By the treaty's terms the Sisseton and Wahpeton Dakota ceded to the government all claims to their lands in Minnesota in exchange for $1,665,000 (Folwell [1921] 1956, 281; Meyer 1967, 80). Two years after the treaty was signed, officials assigned Mazomani's community to move to the Upper Sioux reservation on the Minnesota River near the Lac qui Parle mission, where another Wahpeton community already lived (Hughes 1927, 61). We found little evidence of Wahpeton presence at Little Rapids after that time.

In 1887, archaeologist Theodore H. Lewis conducted the first archaeological survey of the site. Publication of his map and description of Little Rapids in 1911 initiated a long history of destructive digging by artifact collectors that persisted until we began our excavations nearly one hundred years later.

Each of the groups of people drawn to Little Rapids over the last two centuries brought with it conflicting perspectives and interests. These have permeated relations between Dakota and non-Dakota people to this day.

FEW BIOGRAPHICAL DETAILS about the Indian people of Little Rapids have survived. Most chroniclers of the time did not know Dakota people or their language well. Viewing Indians as inferiors, they wanted the Indians' furs, land, or cultural conversion, not their individual or family histories. Several sources, however, mention Mazomani as a chief at Little Rapids, including an 1834 census by Indian agent Lawrence Taliaferro and a report by missionary Samuel W. Pond (Babcock 1945, 140; Pond [1908] 1986, 6; Hughes [1927] 1969, 65–70; Bray and Bray 1976, 45). One of several Dakota leaders who signed the 1851 treaty, Mazomani traveled to Washington, D.C., seven years later with another Dakota delegation (FIG. 15) to sign the treaty of 1858 (Hughes [1927] 1969, 65; Meyer 1967, 88–108). This treaty specified terms for allotments of reservation lands to the Dakota and left payment of funds to the discretion of the president of the United States. Historian Roy W. Meyer observed that the treaty was an "astonishing document" that "granted the government virtually carte blanche to do as it pleased with them [the Dakota] and their property" (Meyer 1967, 104).

Mazomani, in addition to being a chief who signed several treaties, also led one of the Wahpeton's four Wakan Wacipi or medicine dance groups (Skinner 1920, 263). According to an elderly South Dakota woman named Taisnahotewin (Mrs. Gray-Shawl), a contemporary of Mazomani, the Wakan Wacipi comprised four bands named for their leaders: Iyangmani (Running Walker), H'oka (Singer), Wakanhdi Inyanka (Fast Lightning), and Mazomani. It is possible that the two roles were facets of a single leadership role.

Equally shadowy in the written records are Mazomani's family and other Little Rapids residents. Several sources mention his brothers, Mazasha (Red Iron) and Anptuxa (Red Day), but neither lived at Little Rapids (Hughes [1927] 1969, 65). The community roles played by the other three hundred or so people who inhabited the village in

FIG. 15. Mazomani, photographed in Washington, D.C., 1858

FIG. 16. Mazaokiyewin (Isabel Roberts) working a hide, 1937

the 1830s have been obscured, although traces of them still remain (Bray and Bray 1976, 45; Schoolcraft 1853, 612). The tools they made and used, the ornaments they wore, the foods they prepared and ate, the earth they walked on, and the holes they excavated and later filled remind us of them, though anonymously.

Knowledge about Mazaokiyewin comes only through her great-grandson, Chris Cavender, and her granddaughters, Elsie Cavender and Carrie Schommer. The family's oral history does not indicate whether Mazaokiyewin or her mother, Hazawin, ever lived at Little Rapids, but Dakota people still remember that Mazaokiyewin's hide-working skills were well known in the Upper Sioux Community (Elsie Cavender, personal communication, August 6, 1987). While writing the story inspired by the awl handle, I did not know this about Mazaokiyewin, but shortly afterward, Carrie sent me a photograph showing Mazaokiyewin as an elderly woman working a hide with a bone fleshing tool (FIG. 16). A Minneapolis photographer and collector of Indian artifacts, Monroe P. Killy, had taken the photograph of her in 1937, when she was well into her nineties (personal communication, July 10, 1987).

While the records yield only sketchy profiles of Dakota people, they provide considerable detail about the Euro-Americans who visited Little Rapids in the nineteenth century. Faribault, a well-known figure in fur trade history (FIG. 17), operated winter posts at Little Rapids intermittently for almost a half century between 1802 and 1847, although other men also had licenses to trade there during this period (Pond [1908] 1986, 22; Minnesota Historical Society, n.d.; Gilman 1970, 127). Historians Return I. Holcombe and William H. Bingham seemed certain that Faribault "also passed many portions of the summer at the Rapids" (Holcombe and Bingham 1915, 202).

Faribault may have mediated relations between the Wahpeton community and the missionaries who visited Little Rapids in hopes of being allowed to establish a mission station there. Considering the longevity of his operations in the area, he must have enjoyed amicable relations with the community. Faribault probably strengthened his connection to Little Rapids by his marriage to Pelagie Hanse, the twenty-two-year-old widow of a former superintendent of Indian affairs and the mixed-heritage daughter of trader François Kinnie. She and Faribault had several children, and through her, he would have acquired knowledge about Dakota language and culture, further enhancing his role as cultural middleman at Little Rapids (Holcombe and Bingham 1915, 200).

By the 1820s and 1830s relationships between Dakota people and Euro-Americans had begun to disintegrate, however. As the center of the fur trade shifted to the west, Euro-Americans began eyeing Dakota lands for settlement, and, in part to facilitate this process, missionaries set out to "civilize" and convert the Indians. Military outposts such as Fort Snelling at the confluence of the Minnesota and

FIG. 17. Jean B. Faribault as an older man, about 1860

Mississippi rivers protected the waning fur trade and established "order" for American settlers who began arriving in ever-increasing numbers.

Years after missionary Stephen Riggs visited Little Rapids with his wife in June 1843 (FIG. 18), he recalled their visit this way:

> The bottoms of the Lower Minnesota were putting on their richest robes of green, and the great, wild rose gardens were coming into full perfection of beauty when in the month of June, our barge,

FIG. 18. Stephen Return Riggs and Mary Longley Riggs, about 1850

laden with mission supplies, was making its way up to Traverse des Sioux. At what was known as "The Little Rapids," was a village of Wahpaton [*sic*] Dakotas, the old home of the people at Lac-qui-parle [*in 1880*]. There were certain reasons why we thought that might be the point for the new [mission] station. We made a halt there of half a day, and called the chief men. But they were found to be too much under the influence of the Treaty Indians below [*Dakota people living farther east who had come to distrust the U.S. government*] to give us any encouragement. In fact, they did not want missionaries (Riggs [1880] 1969, 99–100).

For the Dakota, historian Roy W. Meyer wrote, the years 1830 to 1862 were "a period of crisis that was to last thirty years and end

in catastrophe" (Meyer 1967, 48). The rapid acceleration of white settlement in the area and the persistent attempts by the government to
gain permanent control of Dakota land through treaties eventually
precipitated the Dakota War of 1862. According to historian Black
Thunder, the conflict reflected the failure of the government to honor
the terms of various treaties and the Dakota people's opposition to
forced relocation and culture change (Black Thunder et al. 1975, 31–35).

The resistance of the people at Inyan Ceyaka Atonwan to missionary Riggs reflected this growing tension, which may also have been
tied to Mazomani's role as a leader of the medicine dance. He and
others might have refused Riggs's offer in order to protect their spiritual
way of life which, along with their land and resource base, seemed
jeopardized.

As a missionary, Riggs competed directly with Mazomani for
spiritual leadership of the people at Little Rapids. Although Riggs did
not mention the medicine lodge or dance on his visit, he commented
elsewhere on the subject of Dakota religion, noting that "the unknown
and unknowable form a broad belt in which humbuggery can be prac-
ticed by the Dakotas as well as other nations" (Riggs 1893, 214). Dakota
religious institutions did not stand on equal ground with his own.

Fellow missionary Samuel Pond admitted candidly in his description of the medicine dance that he "was never initiated into its
mysteries." He continued, "The ceremonies attending the wakan-dance
were in part the most imposing and in part the most absurd of any
witnessed among the Dakotas" (Pond [1908] 1986, 93).

Opportunities for misunderstanding between Dakota people and
Christian missionaries arose in secular contexts as well. Extending
beyond conversion to Christianity, the missionary agenda sought
changes in Dakota marriage practices and family life, in the division
of labor, and in gender roles. Missionaries and government agents con-
tinually tried to convince Indian men to take up agriculture, disre-
garding the fact that from a Dakota perspective, farming was women's
work. Most Dakota resisted change in gender roles and identities, with
the notable exception of Cloud Man (Mahpiya Wichashta), a Dakota
who willingly experimented with Euro-American farming (Pond [1908]
1986, 11).

Samuel Pond, who arrived in Minnesota in 1834 with his brother
Gideon to work among the Dakota, knew Cloud Man when he
lived near Lake Calhoun at Eatonville (now in Minneapolis), an

"experiment at farming" established in 1829 by Indian agent Taliaferro. According to Pond, Cloud Man was the only chief "decidedly in favor of abandoning the chase and cultivating the arts of civilized life." Believing that Dakota men should turn their attention to agriculture and "adopt the customs of civilized people," Cloud Man tried to "persuade others to adopt his views, but with no success," reported Pond. The missionaries found Cloud Man exemplary; his Dakota contemporaries did not (Meyer 1967, 50; Pond [1908] 1986, 10, 11).

Nineteenth-century documentary sources are consistent and often specific when describing the work roles of Dakota men and women. Although their authors differed in their attitudes toward the Dakota, they mutually observed the great volume of work performed by women (C. Eastman [1902] 1971; M. Eastman 1853; Pond [1908] 1986; Riggs 1893).

Fur trader Philander Prescott, an interpreter for the U.S. government in the 1840s, described the Dakota division of labor this way: "The men hunt a little in summer, go to war, kill an enemy, dance, lounge, sleep, and smoke. The women do every thing—nurse, chop wood, and carry it on their backs from a half to a whole mile; hoe the ground for planting, plant, hoe the corn, gather wild fruit, carry the lodge, and in winter cut and carry the poles to pitch it with; clear off the snow, etc., etc.; and the men often sit and look on" (Prescott 1852, 188).

Observers repeatedly and in varying degrees of approval or disapproval described the strength and industry of Dakota women. Typical in tone was the comment of historian and minister Edward D. Neill: "Dahkotah females deserve the sympathy of every tender heart. From early childhood they lead 'worse than a dog's life.' . . . They are the hewers of wood, and the drawers of water for the camp. . . . How few of the gentle sex properly appreciate the everlasting obligations they are under to the Son of Mary, after the flesh, who was the first that taught the true sphere and the true mission of woman!" (Neill 1858, 82–83).

Pond's description of Dakota gender roles and relations as he viewed them in 1834 shows a degree of cultural relativism unusual for the time. With fascination he noted differences in men's and women's swimming techniques, for example, commenting that women "in everything they did had a fashion of their own, differing from that of the men." Evaluating their division of labor, he wrote:

White visitors to an Indian village, seeing the women carrying wood a few rods, wrote down for the information of the public that the lazy men compelled their wives to carry all the burdens; but while the woman was carrying the wood, her husband perhaps, after a weary day spent in pursuing game, was bringing it home on his back a distance of five or ten miles. When the Dakota women were told that the men made them do all the work, they laughed for they knew better. They did much that is not considered appropriate for civilized women, but there was little that would be considered appropriate work for white women to do (Pond [1908] 1986, 155, 49).

Few early nineteenth-century Dakota women left records of their attitudes toward the missionaries and their idea that men should plant corn, but Dakota-authored texts suggest that the Indians found *wasicun* (Euro-American men) strange. Charles Eastman's youthful impressions of "praying men," fur traders, military men, and government officials indicated that he and other Wahpeton people found Euro-American ideas mysterious, unthinkable, and at times simply humorous (Riggs 1890, 536; C. Eastman [1902] 1971, 239–47).

Lack of understanding, failure to keep treaty promises, and escalating tensions between Dakota people and new settlers in Minnesota finally erupted into the brief Dakota War of 1862. Crowded onto a narrow strip of land along the south side of the Minnesota River and desperate for food while government leaders focused their attention on the Civil War, several young Dakota men killed a family of white settlers, beginning a bloody conflict that many Dakota knew to be hopeless. Although only some Dakota participated in or supported attacks on white farmers, all Dakota people suffered. Historian Meyer distilled the essence of this tragedy, which resulted in removal of Minnesota's Dakota people to reservations in what are now South Dakota, Nebraska, and North Dakota:

Whatever the end of the Sioux Uprising may have meant to the white man—a chance to speculate in land or acquire a farm in lands previously unavailable— . . . for the Sioux it meant just one thing: catastrophe. It meant their expulsion from the land where they and their ancestors had lived since the immemorial past, and, more than that, it meant the shattering of whatever unity the Santee [*Eastern Dakota*] bands had possessed. Never again were the Mdewakantons, Wahpekutes, Sissetons, and Wahpetons one people, occupying a single fairly well defined land area. Henceforth they were scattered over states and provinces, with hundreds of miles separating their dispersed settlements and the lands between rapidly filling up with white men, who learned eventually to tolerate the Indian, if only to exploit him, but never to accept him as an equal (Meyer 1967, 132).

According to Dakota oral tradition, Mazomani had tried to make peace during the conflict. A marker placed near his grave in Upper Sioux Agency State Park near Granite Falls reports that he was wounded during the Battle of Wood Lake "by white soldiers while carrying a flag of truce as he tried to enter their camp to arrange for the release of captives." His followers carried him to a nearby village, where he died early the following morning, September 23, 1862, "after embracing his wife and daughter, and telling them: 'I love you very much. But I am going to leave you now.'" The marker notes that after the 1862 war, his daughter, Mazaokiyewin, was among the many Dakota people exiled to the barren Crow Creek Reservation in present-day South Dakota. Known as Isabel Roberts, she apparently returned to Minnesota's Granite Falls area in the 1880s or later with other Dakota exiles, where she became a leading member of the Upper Sioux community. Many of Roberts's descendants continued to live in the area (historical marker, written with the assistance of Elsie Cavender and placed by the Minnesota Historical Society).

IN 1854, EIGHT YEARS before Mazomani's death and shortly after the treaty and dispersal of the Wahpeton from Inyan Ceyaka Atonwan, U.S. Deputy Land Surveyor Henry B. Walsh arrived at Little Rapids to map the area in anticipation of future land sales. Walsh noted that the "land in this Township is generally of 1st rate quality—& for the most part level. It is well timbered with . . . elm, oak, ash and maple &c. and has numerous small prairies at intervals throughout. . . . There are a number of settlements and farms already opened" (Walsh 1854). From Walsh's survey notes and maps, one would never suspect that Indian people ever lived or raised corn at

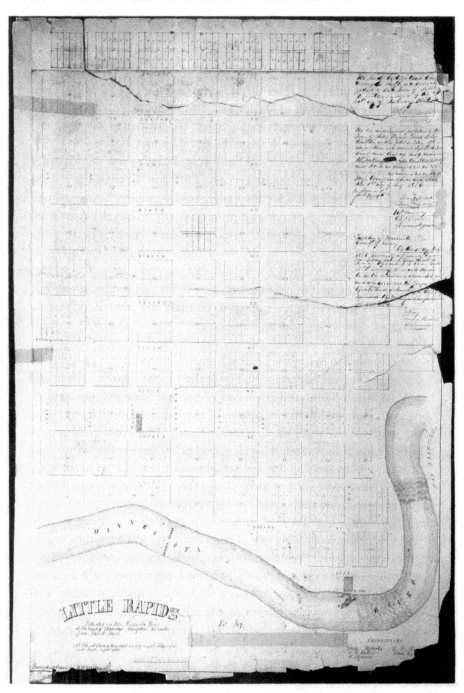

FIG. 19. Plat map, Little Rapids, 1856; north is to the left.

Little Rapids. A map notation, "Indian graves," tells only that they died there.

By 1856 land surveyors had platted lots for a proposed "Town of Little Rapids," with streets numbered First through Twelfth moving east in regular intervals from the river intersected by Oak, Elm, Ash, Maple, Chestnut, Walnut, Pine, and Laurel avenues (FIG. 19). This never-settled town appears on a Scott County map of 1858, but thereafter, maps show only farms in the vicinity.

Archaeologists first observed Little Rapids only a few decades after the Wahpeton left. On August 24, 1887, Theodore Lewis surveyed the site (Winchell 1911, 191). Like the earlier land surveyors, Lewis seemed unaware of the once-active community at Inyan Ceyaka Atonwan. Reflecting the archaeological preoccupations of the period, he focused entirely on the "tumuli"—the burial mounds—and an oval-shaped enclosure formed by a low earthen wall or embankment (FIG. 20). Seeing no connection between them and the Indian people who had lived there in the not-so-distant past, he attributed them to a more advanced "mound-builder" race—"a vanished people entirely different from the Indians" (Keyes 1928, 103).

According to this popular nineteenth-century theory, people related to prehistoric Mexicans had built the mounds in the eastern and central United States and then had either withdrawn southward or been exterminated by the ancestors of the American Indians (Trigger 1980, 665). "The latter, more popular claim," observed archaeologist Bruce Trigger, "reflected the widespread belief [among Euro-Americans] that the Indians were genocidal savages and made the archaeological record appear to be further justification for waging of war upon them and the seizure of their land" (Trigger 1980, 665–66).

Lewis's work at Little Rapids was part of the extensive North-western Archaeological Survey of eighteen states and Manitoba organized by Alfred J. Hill (Winchell 1911, vi–xiv; Keyes 1928, 96–108, 146–55). In the 1860s Hill, a civil engineer, became a member of the Minnesota Historical Society and later chaired its archaeology committee, collecting information about mounds and other "antiquities" in the area. In 1880 he met Lewis, who undertook the field surveys to locate the rapidly disappearing archaeological sites.

Lewis had been a teacher in Ohio, where he "acquired his liking for archaeological research, and likewise his ideas as to the distinctness of the 'mound builder' from the modern Indian" (Winchell 1911, x).

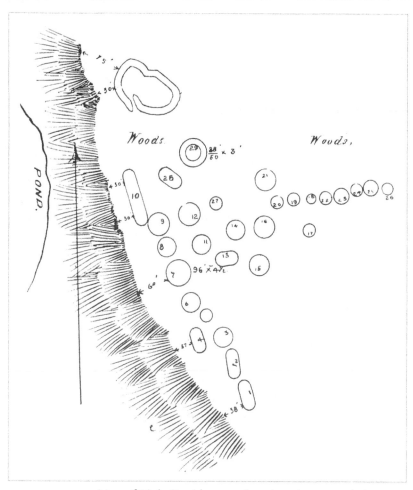

FIG. 20. Map of Little Rapids mounds and enclosure made by Theodore Lewis

He moved to St. Paul in 1878. Between 1881 and 1895 he reportedly traveled nearly fifty-four thousand miles, more than ten thousand on foot, to complete the survey (Keyes 1920, 96).

Lewis's silence about the Wahpeton community at Little Rapids is unsurprising, given his beliefs about the origins of burial mounds and other earthworks. Even if he saw traces of the abandoned village, he would not have associated them with the burial places or the enclosure. Lewis and his contemporaries did not believe Indians were capable of designing or constructing such complex features as mounds, a perspective suggesting the deep chasm that has separated Indian people from archaeologists since the earliest years of the profession.

Ironically, at the time Lewis was conducting his survey, the Reverend Edward Ashley, a missionary in the mid-1880s at the Devils Lake reservation in present-day North Dakota, apparently spoke with elders about "Inyan ceyaka atonwan, Village at the Rapids." It was probably on Ashley's authority that Riggs wrote in 1893 that "old men still living" in the 1880s remembered when the Wahpeton "established their planting village at what has been called Little Rapids, on the lower part of the Minnesota River" (Riggs 1893, 158, 180). While these elders might have been able to tell Lewis something about the burial mounds and the enclosure, he would never have thought to ask them, given his prejudices and assumptions.

Debates about mounds and other earthworks throughout North America dominated the early development of professional archaeology and continue to shape the field today. In the early 1900s some archaeologists still attributed these constructions to non-Indian mound-builders, but as more extensive studies were undertaken, most professionals came to believe that the mounds were built by Indian people. The newer theories often condescendingly suggested, however, that the mounds were built relatively recently and did not reflect significant cultural complexity or achievement (Trigger 1980, 666).

PROFESSIONAL ARCHAEOLOGISTS HAVE not been the only people interested in the mounds and the material goods buried in them. Less scrupulous visitors dug at these sites to collect artifacts for sale in the thriving international market in antiquities. As early as 1906 the federal government, supported by professional archaeologists, attempted to pass legislation to prevent the wholesale destruction of archaeological sites by artifact collectors. The Preservation of American Antiquities Act passed that year (34 Stat. 225) makes it a federal crime to "appropriate, excavate, injure or destroy any . . . object of antiquity situated on lands owned or controlled by the Government of the United States" without the permission of the government (S. Moore 1989, 202).

This same act, it has recently been noted, effectively defined "dead Indians located on federal lands as archaeological resources and converted them to federal property," further exacerbating tensions between Indians and anthropologists (Monroe and Echo-Hawk 1991, 57). Not surprisingly, Indian people resented the continuing disrespectful treatment of their sites by professional archaeologists and physical anthropologists, as well as by amateur diggers (Deloria 1989; Moore 1989; Zimmerman 1989; Monroe and Echo-Hawk 1991). Accordingly, since the 1960s Indians have called for legislation prohibiting the disturbance of sacred sites by archaeologists and have demanded the "repatriation" or return to Indian people of remains already excavated.

Vine Deloria, Jr., and other Indians lobbying for this legislation view the archaeologists' detached, scientific approach to Indian skeletal remains as a lingering legacy of earlier Euro-American oppression. They argue that archaeologists and physical anthropologists, who learn little from their studies, would never consider nor be permitted to use the bones of any other American racial, ethnic, or economic group for such questionable purposes (Deloria 1989, 2). Suzan S. Harjo, director of the Morning Star Foundation, has expressed the view held by many Indians about the necessity of reburying the archaeological remains held by many museums. "We need to declassify Indian people as archaeological resources of the United States. . . . Anthropologists and archaeologists, like pot diggers or grave robbers, have made us a commodity. We want recognition of Indians as human beings with human rights" (Johnson 1990, 14).

Indians and their supporters, including some archaeologists, have succeeded in winning new legislation to address this situation. Passed in 1990, the Native American Graves Protection and Repatriation Act (104 Stat. 3048) has been described as

> the most important human rights legislation ever passed by Congress for Native Americans . . . because it provides them equal rights regarding their dead. It recognizes that scientific rights of inquiry do not automatically take precedence over religious and cultural beliefs; it provides a mechanism for return of objects that were not acquired with the consent of rightful owners; and it creates an opportunity for Native Americans and . . . [scientists] to work in partnership together (Monroe and Echo-Hawk 1991, 55).

Although the mounds at Little Rapids have never been excavated by professional archaeologists, publication in 1911 of Lewis's survey map and description made it possible for eager amateur archaeologists and collectors to visit the site. Some obviously went there because of the mounds, as evidenced by the still-gaping holes they left. None of the amateurs encountered during our investigation in the 1980s admitted to digging in the mounds, knowing that this was prohibited by Minnesota law.[6]

Records of amateur archaeology at Little Rapids date to the 1930s. At that time the privately owned site first captured the attention of a group of people who were to visit and dig there for two decades (Klammer and Klammer 1935, 1949; Brown 1937). Kenneth K. and Paul W. Klammer, the father-and-son team who led these expeditions, appreciated the historical significance of the materials they found. They excavated numerous items associated with the fur trade and felt confident that they had discovered traces of a trading post north of the mounds and enclosure (FIG. 21). The Klammers saw the site as a potential laboratory for studying "the cultural transition that was taking place among the native inhabitants of the region during the time the post was in use, and the mingling of Indian and white culture traits. . . . From the evidence gathered, it seems clear that thoroughgoing excavation would furnish much knowledge of what was clearly an important community" (Klammer and Klammer 1949, 30).

To "protect it as far as possible against idle curiosity hunters," the Klammers kept the location of the site secret but tried to interest professional archaeologists in it (Brown 1937). In 1941 University of Minnesota archaeologist Lloyd A. Wilford visited the site with the Klammers. In 1951 and 1952 he failed to find it again, apparently because roads into the area were flooded. It is not clear from Wilford's notes if he planned to excavate the site (Wilford 1941, 1951, 1952, 1956).

Other professional archaeologists followed Wilford to Little Rapids. Their records mention the site's historical significance and its disturbance by collectors. By the late 1970s, according to one report, Little Rapids had been "severely potted" (MHS 1977). Some collectors using metal detectors found hoes, axes, knives, kettles, traps, and other metal goods originally exchanged with local Indians for furs. Like coin or stamp collectors, these amateurs collected fur trade objects as a

---

6. As far as we know, the collectors whom we consulted dug at Little Rapids while the land was privately owned and before passage of state and federal laws prohibiting such digging.

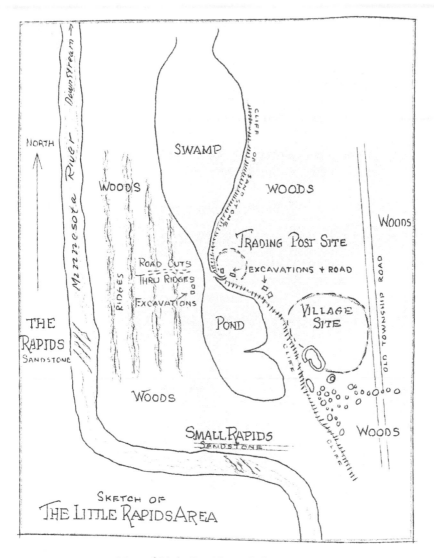

FIG. 21. Map of Little Rapids made by Kenneth K. and Paul Klammer, 1949

hobby, but as we later learned, in the process they frequently made professional exploration of the site difficult.

One collector acknowledged extensive digging at Little Rapids. In 1972 a local newspaper revealed his claim to have located and excavated Faribault's trading post, down to its white ceramic doorknob

(Gustafson 1972, A9). When I later reviewed his notebooks and photographs, I found them undecipherable, indicating neither where he dug, how he excavated, the location of his finds, nor the basis for his interpretations.

Unauthorized digging was still under way when we tested the site in 1979 to determine whether it was sufficiently intact to warrant systematic excavation. In my preliminary work, I contacted some of the collectors identified by Department of Natural Resources personnel and the archaeologists who had visited the site in the 1970s. The collectors eagerly showed me where they had dug and what they had found and offered to help locate promising excavation areas with their metal detectors.

One collector told me a story about an experience at Little Rapids. He confided that after he had been reprimanded by a professional archaeologist who found him digging near the mounds, the collector retaliated by burying a South American clay figurine in one of the mounds.

His story suddenly brought to mind an incident I had forgotten and never associated with Little Rapids. In the mid-1970s someone brought a small ceramic figurine to the university's anthropology department for analysis, claiming that it had been found in a southern Minnesota mound. The three of us who looked at it unanimously agreed that it had come from Central or South America and could not have been locally made. What was it doing in a Minnesota mound? Fleeting fantasies of newspaper headlines announcing a major archaeological breakthrough—"Evidence of Long Distance Trade between Ancient Minnesotans and Ancient Meso-Americans!"—passed through our minds.

Eventually the piece went to the Smithsonian Institution for more expert identification. The collector's confession a few years later solved this minor archaeological mystery. A century earlier, Hill and Lewis might have accepted the figure as evidence in support of their mound-builder theories. In contrast, the Wahpeton elders at Devils Lake, and some of their contemporary descendants, would have found the intruder's exploitation of the mounds outrageous. The clash of cultures has continued at Little Rapids.

FIVE

CYCLES
OF THE
MOONS

P EOPLE INTERESTED IN the past find the notion of traveling through
time compelling. They flock to reconstructed sites such as
Colonial Williamsburg, nineteenth-century Historic Fort Snelling, and
hundreds of other "living-history" museums across the country. There,
costumed interpreters re-create the activities, sights, sounds, smells,
and ambience of the past. As critics have pointed out, however, these
renderings often reflect the perspectives of a narrow segment of the
population—white southerners, not slaves; the economic elite, not
the working classes; European colonists, not Indian people (Wallace
1981, 63–96; Blakey 1983, 11).

The impulse to feel the past—to imagine what life might have
been like—is particularly strong when we study the history of Indian
people who left no written records or were described by outsiders with
little understanding of Indian ways of life. In the words of Indian author
D'Arcy McNickle, the consequence of this limited knowledge "was
to place in the hands of strangers, invariably misinformed, often hostile,
the delicate task of transmitting to the world information about one
of its major population groups" (McNickle 1972, 29).

When teaching archaeology, I sometimes place students in small
groups and ask them to imagine that a technological breakthrough has
allowed them to travel back in time and to observe people previously
known to us primarily through archaeological records or the writings
of outsiders. I ask the students to describe where they would go; the

time period they would investigate; the questions, issues, and topics they would address in their hypothetical study; and how their project might resolve a current debate in archaeology or expand current understanding about the past.

The point of this exercise is to engage students' archaeological imaginations—to stretch their thinking about people in the past and to counter the limitations of many written sources. I want them to appreciate the constraints of knowledge based on fragmentary remains, to expand their thinking about what they would like to know, and to face some of the problems of crossing time and cultural barriers.

The notion of time travel is especially appealing in the case of Little Rapids because the sense of the place and the time expressed in written records is so exclusively Euro-American. Most chroniclers described the natural environment, climate, soil conditions, mineral resources, water supplies, and topography, noting in particular the transportation routes and economic opportunities that would interest potential settlers. Some writers focused on Indian leadership and warfare, topics that by the 1830s were embedded in the highly charged context of treaty negotiations and military logistics to force Indians off their lands and onto reservations. Other writers focused on the size and location of Indian communities, Indian settlement patterns, and Indian subsistence practices. Many accounts emphasized the perceived inability of Indians to support themselves. Indians would be better off, these writers argued, if they would adopt European ways or enter the protective custody of the U.S. government.

Indian agent Lawrence Taliaferro's 1839 report to the Indian affairs commissioner about the "East Wahpeeton" at Little Rapids was typical:

> This fractional band number 325 souls . . . [they] are poor and miserable, raise but little corn, and their dependence upon the chase precarious and doubtful . . . as their game is at an end. Their *fate is sealed,* and *they are anxious for a treaty with the Government;* and I believe it to be the only means whereby this remnant of people may be saved much suffering and certain destruction in a very few years from want and sickness (Taliaferro 1839, 495).

While this kind of description may have served Taliaferro's interest in preparing the way for white settlement, our excavations at Little Rapids suggest a more viable existence.

Documentary references to Little Rapids are usually sketchy, perhaps because the site was set back from the Minnesota River transportation route or because the Wahpeton people living there did not welcome visits from intruders. Riggs's brief account of his 1843 visit suggests that the latter might be true (Riggs [1880] 1969, 100–101).

Riggs also mentioned Little Rapids in his report on Dakota grammar and ethnography. He wrote: "The Wahpetonwan, *Village in the Leaves,* probably obtained their name from the fact that formerly they lived only in the woods. The old home of this band was about the Little Rapids. . . . [Forty] years ago it was written: 'About 300 still reside there, but the larger part of the band have removed to Lac-qui-parle and Big Stone Lake' " (Riggs 1893, 157). Another reliable source of first-hand information on the Wahpeton community was Joseph N. Nicollet, a French scientist who led two government-sponsored exploratory expeditions in the area. Nicollet visited Little Rapids on June 11, 1838, and wrote: "Village of the Little Rapids, 15 lodges . . . these are the people of the leaf (the *Warhpetonwan*) of whom the chief is *Maza Omanki*—who walks or who will get himself in iron. The other parts of this tribe are at Lac qui Parle and at Big Stone Lake." Nicollet called the village "Inyan cheaka," or "the barrier of stone," which was most likely a reference to the rapids in the river (Bray and Bray 1976, 45, 256).

Fur trade records contain some references to Little Rapids but only limited detail about Dakota people (La Bathe 1828; Faribault 1833). They include, however, a good deal of information about goods issued to traders by the American Fur Company for exchange with Indian people (FIG. 22). These trade goods—broken, lost, or intentionally buried underground—make up the largest component of archaeological artifacts found at Little Rapids (FIG. 23).

To offset the Eurocentric and imprecise qualities of the written documents and to acquire a better grasp of the times, I sometimes imagine being transported into the past by a bilingual, bicultural, bitemporal guide—a Dakota person willing and able to explain to me his or her view of the area's politics, tensions, and interactions. The closest I could come to this at Little Rapids was to combine available sources—archaeological, written, oral, and pictorial—to identify some of the things we might have seen and known had we been in the vicinity of Little Rapids in the 1800s.

"LITTLE RAPIDS" HAS BEEN a place name for at least two centuries. Most fur trade accounts refer to trading posts there by that name, although for a brief period American Fur Company personnel called it "Fort Confederation" (Taliaferro 1826). By the 1830s government officials included Little Rapids as part of the Northwestern Agency headquartered at St. Peter's or Mendota (Taliaferro 1839, 493–98). Most people, Dakota and non-Dakota, living in the territory at this time would have known the name, size, and location of the area's Dakota communities. According to Riggs, the Wahpeton council fire included the following bands: "(1) Inyan ceyaka atonwan, *Village at the Rapids;* (2) Takapsin tonwanna, *Those who Dwell at the Shinny-ground* [*sic*]; (3) Wiyaka otina, *Dwellers on the Sand;* (4) Otehi atonwan, *Village On-the-Thicket;* (5) Wita otina, *Dwellers In-the-Island;* (6) Wakpa atonwan, *Village On-the-River;* (7) Can-kaga otina, *Dwellers In-Log* (huts?)" (Riggs 1893, 158).

The names imply autonomous communities, although, as Riggs explained, they represented descent groups, not necessarily residential groups. The size and character of Dakota communities fluctuated over the course of a year, depending on the season's activities. While people probably most often lived with relatives, members of the Dakota alliance visited each other and seem to have resided in mixed communities.

Before I tried to visualize specific kinds of Dakota encampments, my impressions of them were vague and generic. Most nineteenth-century observers and twentieth-century archaeologists labeled almost any Indian community, settlement, or site a "village," regardless of the community's size, composition, or function.

I eventually developed more precise pictures of the array of sites the Dakota used over the course of a year by analyzing women's and men's activity patterns as described in written sources. I supplemented those images with information from nineteenth-century illustrations of Dakota communities. Then, in a kind of reverse archaeology, I imagined the same places as they might appear shortly after people had left them and intentionally or inadvertently abandoned items that might enter the archaeological record as imperishable remnants of their daily lives. I paid special attention to evidence that helped distinguish one kind of site from another rather than to things such as multipurpose tools or ornaments that would appear at every site regardless of season or activities undertaken. Finally, I compared what we actually found at Little Rapids with what would be found at these idealized types of sites.

CHART I Dakota Calendar

Waniyetu (WINTER)
   Witehi wi—the Hard or Severe Moon (January)
   Wicata wi—the Raccoon Moon (February)
   Istawicayazan wi—the Moon of Sore Eyes (March)

Wetu (SPRING)
   Magaokata wi—the Moon When Geese Lay Eggs (April)
   Watopapi wi—the Moon When Streams Are Again Navigable
      (also April)
   Wozupi wi—the Moon for Planting (May)
   Wazustecasa wi—the Moon When Strawberries Are Red and
      When Corn Is Hoed (June)

Mdoketu (SUMMER)
   Canpasa wi—the Moon When Chokecherries Are Ripe and
      Geese Shed Their Feathers (also, Wasunpa wi) (July)
   Wasuton wi—the Moon When Corn Is Gathered, or the
      Harvest Moon (August)
   Psinhnaketu wi—the Moon When Rice Is Laid Up to Dry
      (September)

Ptanyetu (FALL)
   Wazupi wi—the Moon for Drying Rice (October)
   Takiyuha wi—the Moon When Deer Rut (November)
   Tahecapsun wi—the Moon When Deer Shed Their Horns
      (December)

SOURCES: Names adapted from Riggs 1890, 564–65; Prescott 1852, 177, 564.

If we had been in the vicinity of Little Rapids in the 1830s, we could have seen how Dakota sites looked when used in the ways that had sustained the Dakota physically and spiritually for centuries. At that time, the Dakota way of life still revolved around an annual cycle of activities closely tied to seasonally important plants and animals. The cycle is reflected in the names of Dakota *wi,* lunar months (see CHART I), given varying names in nineteenth-century sources, that were divided into four seasons of unequal lengths (Riggs 1893, 165–66; Prescott 1852, 177).

Over the course of the yearly cycle, Dakota encampments varied in size and composition, activities undertaken, and materials manufactured and used. Housing, facilities such as storage areas and drying racks, tools, and clothing were adjusted to prevailing conditions. Seasonal sites looked different from one another in the 1800s and look different archaeologically. A half dozen living sites could have been seen around the landscape at different times of the year.

WILD-RICING AND HARVESTING SITES

In the late summer, a certain coolness returned to the evening and early morning air along the Minnesota River. Just after the women harvested the corn near the planting villages, families packed up their gear and moved to wild-ricing camps. There they set up their tipis on high ground near shallow ricing lakes. While most activities focused on rice harvesting and processing, people also collected blueberries and huckleberries, fished, hunted deer, and shot waterfowl as the birds feasted on ripe grain. Harvest was a season of comfort and plenty, enlivened by social events including a maidens' feast and dances. People consumed quantities of food in preliminary "feasts or offerings in honor of the 'Water Chief,' so that there might not be any drowning accident during the harvest." When it came time to harvest, groups tied the growing grain into bundles and allowed it to stand in the water for a few more days. Then, after ceremonial offerings, canoeists returned to the lake. As one person directed the canoe through the grass, others tapped the heads of the bundles with sticks, knocking the rice into the bottom of the canoe (FIG. 24). Captain Seth Eastman, the frontier artist stationed at Fort Snelling in 1830–31 and the 1840s, portrayed young women harvesting rice wearing earrings identical to ones found at Little Rapids (C. Eastman [1902] 1971, 200–204, M. Eastman 1853, 51-52; Densmore 1954, 21; Pond 1986, 29).

The rice was then dried in the sun or on scaffolds with fires underneath. Next, it was parched by being heated in a kettle over a fire and put into circular pits about two feet deep and two feet wide. Young men washed their feet, put on new moccasins, and trod on the rice in the pits until it was hulled. The women then placed it on a robe that they shook to separate the chaff from the kernels of rice (Eastman [1902] 1971, 202). Rice not immediately consumed was stored in well-concealed pits or caches lined with dry grass and bark.

FIG. 24. Detail from *Gathering Wild Rice,* 1853 engraving after Seth Eastman

DEER–HUNTING ENCAMPMENTS

After the ricing season ended in early October, people dispersed into smaller groups for the fall deer hunt (FIG. 25). Though land was "held in common" by the Dakota, according to Pond, each band hunted in "the part of the country that was accessible from their summer village." Over the next several months, the hunting parties established a series of base camps, moving from one area to another as they exhausted the local deer supply. Since the men hunted along the routes to the camps, they carried little with them other than their traps and weapons. Women, sometimes assisted by dogs or horses, carried everything else—tipi skins, tools, cooking pots, utensils, blankets, and other skins. People usually traveled with few material goods, because a successful hunt meant that they would have heavy loads to transport back to their winter camps in January (Pond [1908] 1986, 44–53).

Arriving at a hunting camp, the women cleared the ground with

FIG. 25. Detail from *Indians Travelling*, 1853 engraving after Seth Eastman

their hoes and collected the usual fourteen poles needed to erect their tipis. Then they gathered dried grass and hay for insulating the tipis inside and outside and wood for heating and cooking. Meanwhile, the men met to plan the next day's hunting areas and to prescribe boundaries in a way designed to ensure "that all might have an equal chance at the game." According to Pond, who observed Dakota practices for many years, "If any one passed the prescribed limits, he ran the risk of having his gun broken" (Pond [1908] 1986, 46).

The Dakota also had rules governing the distribution of meat so that everyone would get some, regardless of their hunting success or failure. Pond described their system this way:

> The Dakotas did not admit that any one had a right to appropriate the whole deer to himself because he killed it. Their rules required that any one who was hunting with others should, on killing a

deer, give notice to any who were within hearing, by a certain shout, the meaning of which was well known. . . . Having given the signal, the hunter waited a while, and if no one came he cut up the deer and carried it home; but if one came, the flesh was equally divided between the two, the one who killed the deer taking the skin. If two or three came, each had a right to a certain portion of the flesh, but only the three who were first to arrive had any claim to it. The one who killed the deer always kept the skin and wrapped up his part of the flesh in it.

With some admiration, Pond observed:

These rules about the division of game were a great encouragement to the less skillful and less able hunters, for, if they killed nothing themselves, they might hope not to return empty; and the rules worked no injury to the more successful, for the families must all be fed, and this plan saved them the labor of carrying the meat home for others (Pond [1908] 1986, 49–50).

If the hunt for deer, or any other game such as bear or raccoon encountered along the way, was highly successful, the men stored the surplus in wooden pens to protect it until they passed by on their return. People remained in each hunting camp for a week or two until most of the animals in the area had been harvested. Then they packed up their belongings, moved on a few miles, and established a new hunting camp, repeating the process several times until snow made travel difficult, severe cold set in, or the deer grew scarce and lean (Pond [1908] 1986, 52).

WINTER CAMPS

In January, as the Minnesota winter turned its coldest, the small hunting parties returned to the vicinity of their summer camps. There they dug in for winter, erecting their tipis in sheltered, wooded areas where they could draw on their reserves of food supplies stored since summer. Corn and other food, according to Pond, had been "put in barrels made of bark . . . and buried until the owners returned from the deer-hunt in January, and was so concealed that, when the snow was on the ground, none but the owners could easily find it." They ate the corn and rice mixed with tallow or animal fat, strips of dried

FIG. 26. Skin lodges like these were used in winter and while traveling. Detail from *Dakotah Encampment,* 1853 engraving after Seth Eastman

venison, and dried roots and berries. Nothing was wasted (Pond [1908] 1986, 27).

Ignoring their nearby gabled summer lodges, people set up tipis for winter housing (FIG. 26). Pond described their winter quarters as:

> made of eight dressed buffalo skins, sewed together with sinews, and when set up . . . of a conical shape, about twelve feet in height, and ten or twelve feet in diameter. . . . In the center of the tent, a space for the first three or four feet square was fenced with sticks of wood, outside of which the ground was covered

FIG. 27. Detail from *Spearing Fish in Winter*, 1853 engraving after
Seth Eastman

with hay, and that was spread over with buffalo robes. . . . When
whole, well set, and warmed by a good fire, the tent or tepee was
tolerably comfortable even in the coldest weather. . . . On the
whole, no better dwelling for summer or winter could be devised
for hunters (Pond [1908] 1986, 38–39).

Pond observed that in the winter months, women "had considerable labor to perform, such as getting wood, dressing deer skins,
making moccasins, etc., but the men had little to do." Men fished
(FIG. 27) and brought furs and skins to traders who gave them manufactured goods in exchange. Mostly, however, the men spent their
time resting, visiting, and gambling. For recreation, men and women
played a ball game similar to their summer lacrosse (FIG. 28). Pond
described the women's game: "They knocked the ball with clubs upon

FIG. 28. *Ball Play on the Ice,* 1853 engraving after Seth Eastman

the ice of a frozen lake or river. Many of them were skillful players, and some were swift runners; but their motions were impeded by their dress. . . . They commonly bet heavily on their games." Boys skied down hills standing on bark sleds and bounced specially shaped sticks on the snow or ice until the brief season of "rest and recreation," as Pond recalled it, passed (Pond [1908] 1986, 53, 116–17).

MAPLE SUGAR CAMPS

From March through May, as the snow melted and the cool spring rains brought the ground back to life, members of Dakota communities again dispersed into work groups. In March, most of the women and children, accompanied by a few older men, moved through the crusty snow to their long-time sugar camps located in large maple groves (FIG. 29). They carried heavy brass and iron kettles with them but otherwise manufactured most of what they needed at the site. During their first few days at the camp, the women made troughs of birch bark

FIG. 29. *Indian Sugar Camp*, 1853 engraving after Seth Eastman

FIG. 30. Detail from *Spearing Muskrats in Winter*, 1853 engraving after
Seth Eastman

or basswood to collect the sap at the tree trunk and one or more hollowed-out log "canoes" to hold the gathered sap. The women also repaired and cleaned the large, oval-shaped bark sugar house in which they had lived and worked the previous season. Then they gathered good supplies of fuel for the fires that were needed to boil down the sap (C. Eastman [1902] 1971, 25; M. Eastman 1853, 74).

When the sap began to flow, women tapped the trees with their axes. Then they collected the sap in bark containers and poured it into the "canoes," from which the kettles were kept filled. Within or just outside the sugar house, the women built a long fire and suspended kettles over it to process the sap. The sap boiled for hours until it became syrup. Boys took charge of the kettles, tending the fire and watching them so they did not boil over. They frequently tested the syrup on the snow, apparently consuming a fair amount in the first few days (C. Eastman [1902] 1971, 27).

The women stored the bulk of the syrup to bring back to their summer villages for feasts, where it would be served with wild rice, parched corn, or dried meat. They made sugar cakes by pouring the boiled syrup into molds made from hollow canes, reeds, or the bills of ducks and geese. They also pulverized and packed some in rawhide cases. Although most work at these camps centered on making the syrup and sugar, boys with bows and arrows hunted small birds, rabbits, chipmunks, and pests drawn to the area by the sugar (C. Eastman [1902] 1971, 25, 27, 28).

MUSKRAT CAMPS

While Dakota women and children lived at the sugar camps, most men were many miles away hunting and trapping muskrats (FIG. 30). Thick muskrat furs collected in the spring months were particularly valuable in the fur trade. As the men left the winter camps for this hunt, they carried little with them except their guns, spears, and traps. The parties established camps near the shallow lakes and marshes where the muskrats lived. The men frequently ate muskrat meat, having neither the time nor ammunition to spend on other game. Pond, who visited one of these camps in 1836, commented on the "carcasses of the slaughtered animals lying everywhere in heaps" with their musky smell permeating the air (Pond [1908] 1986, 54–57).

FIG. 31. *Dakota Village,* 1853 engraving after Seth Eastman

SUMMER PLANTING VILLAGES

By late spring, when the Little Rapids awl story begins, men, women, and children had reunited in their summer planting villages. Dakota summer encampments such as the one at Little Rapids are among the best described in nineteenth-century written records and illustrations (FIG. 31). Because of the size and character of the dwellings, chroniclers often labeled the encampments "permanent villages." Since Dakota people did not reside there throughout the year, this name is misleading, but among the different types of camps, these were perhaps the most long-lived. People apparently returned to them for at least several years (Prescott 1852, 192; 1854, 67).

The concept of a planting village was never adopted by nineteenth-century chroniclers or their twentieth-century counterparts. Only Stephen Riggs used the name, which is particularly apt given the centrality of planting, tending, and harvesting corn during the summer months.

Why was this Dakota term overlooked? Perhaps writers felt that by calling such encampments "planting villages," they would draw attention to two things about the Dakota that many Euro-Americans consistently denied or attempted to change: first, that the Dakota, like the settlers who coveted the Dakota's land, were farmers, not just hunters; and second, that women, not men, farmed the land. Pond, after discussing the agricultural work performed by Dakota women in some detail, nonetheless characterized the Dakota as hunters. In a tellingly titled section of his book comparing Indians with Euro-Americans, "Industry of the Hunter and Farmer Compared," Pond wrote:

> The Dakota was a hunter, descended from a long line of hunters, trained to hunting by precept and example, with all the wisdom of a hunter that could be handed down by tradition or gained by experience. . . . Hence it is not strange that it is so difficult to make anything else of him. To expect him to change at once all his habits, to become a steady, plodding farmer, is as absurd as it would be to expect that his dog, whose ancestors have been trained to hunt deer through a hundred generations, should be suddenly transformed into a docile shepherd dog (Pond [1908] 1986, 66).

Many twentieth-century archaeologists, historians, and other social scientists have similarly tended to emphasize men's activities and perspectives and to accept the nineteenth-century manifest destiny ideology that views Euro-Americans as the land's first farmers.

Following the choice of the Wahpeton elders, however, I refer to Inyan Ceyaka Atonwan as a summer planting village. When the Little Rapids project began in 1979, however, I had never heard that name for the site and had no idea who lived there, when, for how long, or what they did there. That we had probably located portions of Inyan Ceyaka Atonwan, not some other Dakota encampment, became apparent only after analyzing the artifacts and other material remains discovered during three summers of fieldwork and almost a decade of research.

SIX

FIRST
TRACES
UNCOVERED

IN THE ESSAY "Site of Memory," author Toni Morrison described her research strategy for the novel *Beloved* as "literary archaeology":

> On the basis of some information and a little bit of guesswork you journey to a site to see what remains were left behind and to reconstruct the world that these remains imply. What makes it fiction is the nature of the imaginative act: my reliance on the image—on the remains—in addition to recollection, to yield up a kind of truth. By "image" . . . I simply mean "picture" and the feelings that accompany the picture (Morrison 1987, 112).

Using this approach, Morrison wove together slave narratives, stories she heard, and things she read about the past to give voice to black slave women and children who left no written records of their experiences. She retrieved and expressed memories long buried, many of them too terrible for the slave narrators to relate. In the novel she evoked these memories through what she called "material inscriptions": the name "Beloved" carved into a child's gravestone, a character's back scarred from beatings. Each functioned as an "archaeological site or memory trace" which Morrison, like an archaeologist, used to re-create the past (Henderson 1990, 12).

My approach to Little Rapids was something like Morrison's, except that I literally dug in the earth to find what people left behind and what those remains implied about their lives. To get some sense of their world required acts of imagination, the weaving together of evidence from fragmentary sources. Writing about the past, as Morrison put it, requires a mix of "thinking and discovery and selection and order and meaning; it is also awe and reverence and mystery and magic" (Morrison 1987, III).

While Morrison found archaeology to be a useful metaphor to describe her writing process, archaeology at Little Rapids sometimes seemed to me to be like drama or theater. The site was the set for past human actions, emotions, and conflicts; the plot was activated by "the dig," which was a story in itself. The artifacts, like stage props, were material cues of time, place, and culture last used by people living more than a century earlier and brought to life again when twentieth-century excavators touched them.

The action in an archaeological drama takes place on many levels and time frames, not always separable or fully comprehensible. First we had the initial adventure of locating the Little Rapids site. Then we experienced the tension and excitement of organizing each year's dig: assembling an interested and congenial crew, raising funds to support the work, and worrying that the weather would be too hot, too humid, or too stormy.

Actual digging proceeded slowly and undramatically, but the promise and magic of discovery punctuated our days. We always hoped to find some undisturbed, well-preserved key to Dakota community life, something like a time capsule carrying distinctive objects as a record of the time and place. But with the exception of extraordinary sites like Pompeii, frozen in time by volcanic ash, such archaeological discoveries are rare.

At Little Rapids our discovery process also included the search for key written documents. We surveyed libraries and archives for references to Little Rapids. We fantasized about an "ideal" manuscript—a previously undiscovered journal kept by someone who visited Little Rapids, knew community members and their language well, and wrote about the times with insightful detail. These documents, we learned, did not exist.

THE LITTLE RAPIDS PROJECT began in the summer of 1979 with test excavations to evaluate the site's potential for studying nineteenth-century

Dakota life. This included assessing the extent of the damage done by amateur archaeologists and collectors. Our first challenge, however, proved to be finding the site. Initially I attempted to reach it by using written sources alone, instead of contacting people who had been there. I wrongly assumed that the historical site maps and written descriptions would guide us readily to the area of the present-day wildlife refuge where Dakota people and fur traders once lived.

During the first week of August 1979, I hiked through the Carver Rapids Wayside with Robert C. Vogel, a University of Minnesota graduate student in geography interested in fur trade sites. We failed to locate the mound group at the southern boundary of the village site marked so distinctly on the site maps. Several days later I returned to the refuge with two friends, both anthropologists. We started walking along the park trails at about 10:00 A.M. on a hot, muggy morning. The first thing I noted in my field journal for the day, after walking for more than an hour through tall corn that virtually obliterated the trails we were trying to follow, was, "Mosquitoes ferocious."

We took a break in a sheltered hay storage area used by the farmer who rented land in the refuge. By chance, we met Charles T. (Chuck) Kartak, the Department of Natural Resources park manager. I had not known before that this part of the refuge had a manager. After introductions, he willingly took us directly to the site—about five minutes away—in his pickup truck.

Chuck headed north on a dirt road adjacent to the hay storage area, then turned off the track, driving east through a meadow. Turning north again, now on a barely discernible road, Chuck brought us into a wooded area that cut through the eastern edge of the mound group first mapped by Lewis. We stopped briefly to look at two mounds, each showing painful symptoms of recent digging.

Passing between the mounds and out of the woods, we entered an open grassland interrupted by large oaks and scattered clusters of sumac. Johnson's Slough lay about forty feet below us to the west. Several hundred feet beyond, a forest screen blocked from view the Minnesota River and the rapids that gave the place its name (FIG. 32). This was unquestionably the "village site" identified by the Klammers and other collectors.

Within a few days, I secured permission to test the site from William N. Weir, the Department of Natural Resources regional park manager, and made arrangements to get keys for the entrance gates

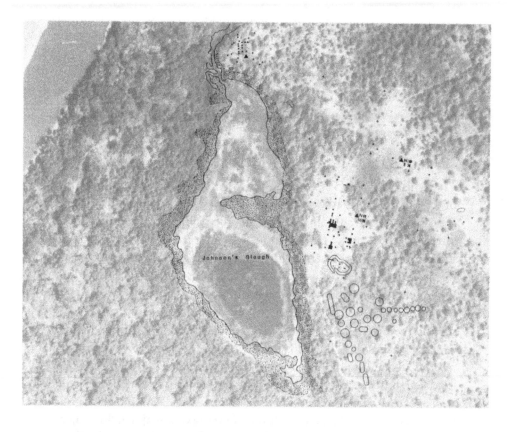

FIG. 32. Aerial view of Minnesota River and Johnson's Slough (left), 1980; enlargement of slough and Little Rapids site (above), with overlay showing excavations and mounds

that limited automobile access to the park's roads. Weir mentioned the history of amateur archaeology and collecting at Little Rapids, noting in particular some extensive digging by collectors in the years Northern States Power Company owned the land.

Personnel from the department, as well as from the U.S. Fish and Wildlife Service, which managed areas of the refuge adjacent to Little Rapids, expressed enthusiasm about the prospect of archaeological research at the site. Several natural history and environmental studies had been undertaken already as part of development plans for the refuge. These plans included restoration of its native prairie and preservation of the notable mix of bottomland, hardwood forest, and wetland areas (USFWS n.d.). Archaeology could add important historical and cultural dimensions to public information and interpretive programs. Each summer of the dig, personnel proved extremely helpful, generously furnishing information, picnic tables, outhouses, brush clearing, and other vital services that supported our work.

For several days over the next few weeks, colleagues and friends volunteered to help test the site to see what evidence of nineteenth-century Dakota daily life remained below the tall grass and trees covering the area. Although it was clear that the archaeological record had not been disturbed by modern plowing or building, evidence of digging by collectors was conspicuous everywhere. From an archaeologist's perspective, it would be pointless to undertake a major field project unless we could first determine that materials from the period still remained in place.

We began the test excavations after designating a large oak tree in the middle of the grassy area about one hundred meters north of the mounds as a temporary "datum." This would be the reference point for measuring and mapping the site's natural and cultural features, including the places collectors had dug, the mounds, the road along the edge of the ridge above the slough, and our test pits.

As we toured the site, we noted the small holes and plugs of earth where collectors had picked up readings on their metal detectors and dug down to investigate. Burrowing gophers had also left small holes and piles of dirt behind. We often found things in the gophers' and the collectors' back-dirt: small glass beads, tiny fragments of burned bone, shell, charcoal, and small pieces of tinfoil and wire, all rejected by the diggers.

We placed seven small test pits north, south, east, and west of the datum tree at varying distances. These pits ranged in size from a half-meter to a meter square, excavated to a depth of about fifty centimeters where we encountered archaeologically sterile soil or bedrock (FIG. 33). We intentionally dug several test units near the amateurs' probings and placed others some distance from them.

Having used a metal detector to test fur trade era sites in Wisconsin, I decided against trying this technique at Little Rapids. First, unlike the recent collectors, we were interested in the full range of materials that Dakota people had used, not just metal goods. The detecting equipment cannot locate plant and animal resources or artifacts made of glass, shell, bone, clay, or stone. Second, these instruments do not discriminate between recent metal objects and those from periods of archaeological interest. One can spend as much time locating bottle caps and foil from chewing gum or cigarette packs as metal goods used in the fur trade. In the end, digging small test pits seemed more efficient and more informative for our purposes.

Our initial tests were promising. Most pits contained some indication of nineteenth-century Dakota activity—charred animal bone, clamshell fragments, charcoal, ash, and artifact fragments. In two units we found undisturbed nineteenth-century fur trade materials between ten and forty centimeters deep: a glass trade bead, European ceramics, and fragments of trade-silver ornaments. This was sufficient evidence for me to suspend testing and begin planning a more systematic excavation.

For four summers—1980, 1981, 1982, and 1986—we excavated the Little Rapids site under the auspices of the field school program of the anthropology department at the University of Minnesota. We raised funds to support the work each year from a variety of sources. Several units of the university—including the summer school, the graduate school, the continuing education and extension program, the educational development program, and the College of Liberal Arts' honors program—provided money for equipment, salaries, and transportation. The Minnesota Historical Society provided some funds for survey work in 1980, and in 1982 Hamline University in St. Paul supported the participation of Barbara H. O'Connell, a professor of anthropology, and a number of students.

During the 1980s, almost one hundred people worked at and came to know something about Inyan Ceyaka Atonwan. The number included field school staff and university archaeology laboratory

FIG. 33. Test pits, 1979, with tree used as temporary datum at top center

supervisors, volunteer workers, and undergraduate and graduate students (APPENDIX 1). Each summer we formed a small community at Little Rapids. Five days a week, a dozen or two of us at a time drove to the site, worked together for a month or so, and then dispersed. These weeks were intense, our attention collectively riveted on the site. We spent almost twelve hours a day together, returning depleted to our other lives at the end of the day.

We each played certain roles at the site. For the first three years I was the project's director, producer, teacher, and writer. Chris Cavender, Ed Cushing, Sara Evans, and Carrie Schommer joined me in designing and teaching the last (1986) field session. Graduate students with archaeology experience served as field and laboratory supervisors. Working with student apprentices, they also analyzed materials in the university's archaeology laboratory during the academic year. Some of the undergraduates continued their involvement and eventually became assistant field and lab supervisors. The student staff members provided crucial conversation, stimulation, insight, and energy as we deliberated about how and where to dig, how to organize materials once we returned to the university, and how to make sense of what we found.

Making up the field crews were graduate, undergraduate, and continuing education students, most but not all majoring in anthropology. Sometimes interested volunteers joined us for short periods. Like casts in community theater productions, crew members varied considerably in their talent and tolerance for the work. Some people loved digging and found the materials we unearthed fascinating. This sustained them through the first awkward days of learning how to excavate an archaeologist's square with the straight walls and level floors that expose subtle soil features. Others quickly found the digging tedious. They hated the blisters, sore muscles, and sweat and became preoccupied with the earthworms, mosquitoes, gnats, snakes, poison ivy, and other distractions common to most digs in Minnesota.

Planning for the first summer field-school season began in the fall of 1979 when we secured formal permission to work at the site from the Department of Natural Resources and the state archaeologist. I wrote proposals for funds, contacted amateur collectors whom park personnel and professional archaeologists identified as familiar with the site, recruited a field supervisor and crew members, and made arrangements to set up a field laboratory.

On June 21, 1980, a week before we began excavating, I toured Little Rapids with Mary K. Whelan, a graduate student who served as the field and laboratory supervisor for the summers of 1980 and 1981, and three of the collectors who knew the site well. They had spent a good deal of time at Little Rapids before it came under Department of Natural Resources management, and they willingly showed us where they had found many objects.

Orienting ourselves by the datum tree, we walked around the site, placing small red flags in the ground at the location of their finds and mapping them. About twenty meters south of datum, near a test pit from the summer before, one of the collectors indicated a spot where he had found metal trade hoes, a musket, gun parts, brass bracelets, tomahawks, and kettle fragments. He told us that another area, near a small depression just west of the datum tree, was "loaded with trade goods" and "lots of fishhooks." One of the men said that he had discovered a complete gun twenty meters northwest of the tree, and somewhat farther away he had found a tomahawk buried about a meter deep. These represented the remnants of food gathering and process- ing activities and the personal belongings that one would expect to find at a nineteenth-century Dakota encampment.

By the end of the day, the collectors, Mary, and I had flagged seven different locations over a very large area bounded on the north by what the collectors believed to be a fur trade post and on the west by the slough. The southern boundary of their activities had been the burial mounds—none of the men admitted to digging there—and they said they had found nothing east of the township section line about 150 meters from the slough.

That evening one collector invited us to his home to see his ar- tifact collection. Mary and I were simultaneously impressed by and worried about the volume and variety of materials he showed us: about 150 metal trade items including gun parts, projectile points, fishhooks, muskrat spears, hatchets, hoes, knives, awl tips, scissors, rings, bracelets, and more. Was anything left behind? If the other collections from the site proved as extensive as this one, the collectors might have removed most of the metal tools and ornaments that the Dakota residents had received from traders for their furs and eventually left behind at the village.

Over the course of the four-season dig, these worries were partly confirmed. Although we discovered a substantial assemblage of materials, it included few large iron or brass items. In 1982 Teresa M. Halloran, a student working on the project for several years, photographed and inventoried the artifacts found at Little Rapids by three collectors (APPENDIX 2). This gave us a far more complete picture of the range of artifacts left at the site than we would have had from our excavations alone. They also reinforced many of the impressions we had formed about nineteenth-century activities at Little Rapids based on the evidence we had recovered.

Two days after the site tour with the collectors, Mary and I planned our excavation strategy. Our first task was to establish a more permanent datum than the oak tree. We selected a point ten meters north and thirty meters east of it on slightly higher ground near the center of an area that I had assigned as our initial excavation grid system (FIG. 34). The permanent reference marker was a brass pipe about three feet long and three-fourths of an inch in diameter. We pounded it into the ground, leaving a foot visible above the surface, set it in concrete, and inscribed a signature in the wet cement: "21Sc27." This national archaeological code indicated that Little Rapids was the twenty-seventh site formally recorded for Scott (Sc) County in Minnesota (state 21). Now we could measure and map every object we found by its distance, direction, elevation, and depth from ground level at the new permanent datum.

Our next step was to decide where to start digging. For this we used a simple random-sampling strategy, a process repeated on several different occasions as we opened up new parts of the site. We did not want to be too strongly influenced by spots identified by the collectors; they were the most likely to be disturbed. We also wanted to resist the temptation to excavate only in open, easy-to-dig grassland areas rather than in more challenging wooded ground. Archaeological materials might occur in either place, and random sampling ensures that all parts of the grid have an equal chance of being selected.

I began the procedure by drawing a map of the 160-meter-square area on graph paper with datum in the center. I partitioned the grid into sixty-four sample units, each 20-meters square and numbered sequentially. After writing sixty-four numbers on slips of paper and placing them in a small bag, Mary and I closed our eyes and selected six numbers. The samples represented about 10 percent of the total area. Then we matched these numbers to the corresponding numbers on the map to indicate where inside the grid we would begin.

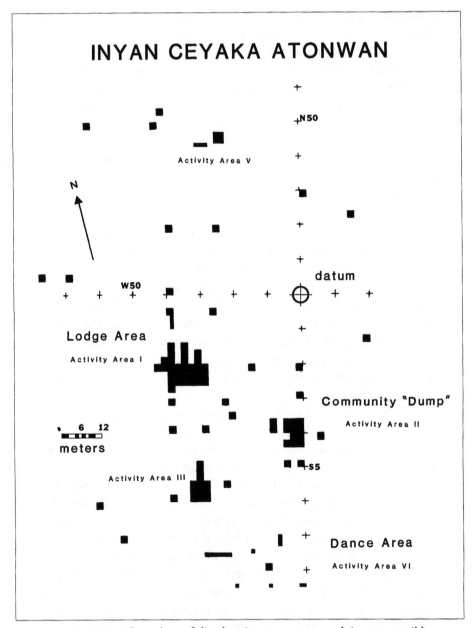

FIG. 34. Overview of dig showing areas excavated (except possible fur post)

Afterward I drew a generic, scale-model sample unit on graph paper and divided it into the one hundred possible two-meter squares contained in each. These were the dimensions of our standard unit of excavation. We numbered these squares sequentially, wrote the numbers one through one hundred on slips of paper, and selected two numbers per sample unit to pinpoint exactly where crew members would dig their first squares.

The following day, we set up a surveyor's transit over our datum. Measuring from there, we placed wooden stakes throughout the grid, labeling each stake's distance and direction from datum. For example, we labeled the stake located ten meters north and twenty meters west of datum "N10/W20." Eventually we outlined the boundaries of our six large sample units and each two-meter square with these stakes, thus transferring our grid system from graph paper to the ground.

By chance, and not surprisingly, given the site's vegetation, several of the units fell in dense brush or woods. They required a good deal of ground clearing by crew members before digging could begin. Other sample units fell in more accessible open areas. To save time and minimize frustration during the first tough days of the field school, I intuitively selected one additional sample unit close to datum in an open area to substitute for one randomly selected wooded unit. Finally we were ready for the field-school students. When they arrived, we assigned two people to work in each of the six sample squares scattered throughout the grid.

Our daily routine in the field followed a regular pattern. We left the university at 7:00 A.M. and usually arrived at the site an hour later. Crew members dug in their two-meter squares, recorded their findings on field forms and in their field journals, or worked in the lab located on a nearby farm until about 4:00 P.M., when we left the site for our return to the university. During the day as we dug or stopped for breaks, we often created scenarios, speculations about why people would have gone to some part of the site and what they would have done to produce the remains—the memory traces—we discovered there.

Some of our ruminations about the Dakota residents were sparked by the summer weather and other environmental conditions. How did they tolerate the exhausting summer heat and humidity and the swarming mosquitoes and gnats? Did they watch the darkening skies some days as we did, hoping to finish our work before a thunderstorm struck? Was their community life, like ours, punctuated

FIG. 35. Starting to dig, 1980

by summer romances and interpersonal tensions, or were such relationships a product of our particular time and place only?

The field teams excavated their two-meter squares from the present ground surface down to archaeologically sterile soil, usually from thirty to fifty centimeters deep (FIG. 35). We worked in ten-centimeter levels, stripping away thin layers of soil within each level, patiently working across the square with trowels and shoveling the loosened dirt into a screen to capture any remains that might have been overlooked.

The size and shape of these excavation units did not relate to any past living or activity area. They simply made it possible to document the location of finds as they were first exposed and then removed from the ground. Digging is a destructive process. Taking materials out of a site without keeping detailed records is like tearing pages from a book without first making a copy. Through our field notes and maps from each level in each unit, we could transfer our findings from the ground to paper. Back in the lab, we were then able to create a facsimile of the site, placing objects in their original spatial, temporal, material, and, eventually, cultural context. These tightly controlled excavation and record-keeping procedures, essential for meaningful historical studies, are an important part of what separates professional from amateur archaeology.

As the excavators uncovered artifacts, plant and animal remains, and traces of structures, they measured and mapped their locations within the squares relative to datum. They also collected soil samples in paper bags in order to recover tiny remains through water flotation and screening techniques. When members of a team completed their square, they took these soil samples and all the other remains to our field lab for processing.

The field lab sat about a mile away from Little Rapids on a farm owned by Jerome Kyllo, a local teacher interested in the site. Students cleaned, counted, and marked each item with an accession identification number indicating exactly where in the grid it was found and that it is housed at the University of Minnesota, which sponsored the dig.

We took some soil samples back to the university for identification and analysis but subjected most to a water flotation and screening process at the field lab. This entailed agitating small amounts of the soil in a container with water. Lightweight materials like charcoal, fish scales and bones, fragments of seeds, corn, and nutshells rise to the top, while heavier silts, sands, bones, and artifact fragments settle to the bottom. As the "light fraction" floats to the surface, it is poured out, dried, and then sorted, identified, and counted. The "heavy fraction" that sinks to the bottom is gently washed through a fine mesh screen, and the remains are dried for identification and analysis.

In 1986 the field-school program differed significantly from that of the three previous summers because it was conducted by a multidisciplinary, multicultural team. Excavation and laboratory routines remained similar, but the crew spent less time at these activities. Instead of digging each day, some student teams went on field trips with our ecologist, Ed Cushing, to study the environment and natural history of the Little Rapids area. They mapped local habitats and the vegetation that the Wahpeton community might have utilized during their summer stay. Carrie Schommer added environmental studies to her language lessons by including Dakota names for plants, animals, and foods. She continued to drill student teams on basic words, numbers, and phrases while they excavated their squares. During our lunch breaks,

Chris Cavender led discussions about Dakota culture and history, including the historic Oceti Sakowin or council fires, contemporary Minnesota Dakota communities, family life, kinship, religion, and philosophy. Then, on Friday mornings, historian Sara Evans helped the group assess the potential and limitations of the primary historical sources we were going through together—fur trader and missionary accounts, Seth Eastman's pictorial records, and Dakota and Euro-American eyewitness reports of the Dakota War of 1862.

This kind of cultural immersion was a new experience for everyone. Those of us with experience in the field seemed to appreciate it even more than the novice crew members who had no basis for comparing our program with a more typical "dig." We found it extraordinary to be able to work collaboratively with people who had direct family ties to the place and the history we were studying. Just as we had fantasized about an ideal document or a key artifact that might reveal elusive aspects of the past, most of us hoped the Dakota participants would have some special knowledge about or insight into the site. But neither Chris nor Carrie, it turned out, was particularly interested in the archaeology or the artifacts. Hearing the Dakota language spoken there each day and learning about Dakota culture from two such knowledgeable teachers, however, immeasurably deepened our appreciation for the site of memory left at Inyan Ceyaka Atonwan.

That the Dakota and other Indian people who came to the site expressed little interest in our excavations was understandable. Given the long history of tensions between Indians and archaeologists, I was grateful simply that Chris and Carrie had agreed to participate in the project. We had not been successful in attracting Indian students to the program, even though we had secured university funding for full tuition scholarships as an incentive. One student's response encapsulated the situation. Several months before the 1986 field school began, Chris and I gave a slide presentation about Little Rapids to students in the university's American Indian studies program in hopes of interesting them in the project. Afterward, a young woman approached us. She said she had been raised in an Indian community that viewed archaeologists as grave robbers. Our presentation contradicted that imagery, she said, and she could see how archaeology could recover unrecorded traces of her own history without disrespect or desecration. Even so, she did not feel able to participate in a field project.

IN OUR FOUR SUMMERS at Little Rapids, we were able to identify the physical boundaries of the nineteenth-century Wahpeton community and to locate the area several hundred meters to the north that might have been the fur trade post mentioned by the collectors and in contemporary written documents. The group of mounds about 100 meters south of datum set the southern boundary of Inyan Ceyaka Atonwan. In the units excavated near the mounds, we found few if any nineteenth-century artifacts, while the number of pre-European contact ceramics and pieces of stone tools increased. At the western edge of the encampment, about 80 meters west of datum, was the crest of the slope running north and south above the slough. Units excavated down the slope toward the slough were generally sterile. Similarly we found little or no archaeological material 80 meters east of datum, again suggesting little activity there. Finally, the units we excavated between 80 and 190 meters north of datum contained few remains until we encountered the boundaries of the possible fur post site, indicated by a dramatic increase in the number of artifacts from the nineteenth and twentieth centuries.

We excavated a total of 103 two-meter-square units within the Wahpeton settlement, approximately 3 percent of the three-and-a-half-acre site area. Although we dug a relatively small portion of the total site, we undoubtedly accumulated a major sample of its imperishable remains. Some areas produced more archaeological materials than others, and we concentrated our excavation efforts in these materially dense parts of the site.

We recovered many traces of Inyan Ceyaka Atonwan: 4,338 artifacts, 32,257 animal remains (Whelan 1987), and more than 11,000 plant remains (Shane 1984). In addition we inventoried over 600 artifacts held in three amateur archaeologists' collections (Halloran 1982). It is not possible to tell precisely what percentage of the community's material goods this represents. We will never know the number of items left behind by the Wahpeton people when they departed the site for the last time, or what proportion perished through natural processes or were taken away by amateur archaeologists and collectors before we began our work. But the traces are sufficient when studied in conjunction with written and visual sources to provide vivid glimpses of life at Little Rapids.

SEVEN

GLIMPSES OF COMMUNITY LIFE

Part I

THE LITTLE RAPIDS DRAMA unfolded slowly, sometimes painfully so, as we exposed and, later, came to understand small fragments of the past. It now seems appropriate that in our field notes and site maps and in our speculative conversations, we abbreviated our names for particularly meaningful activity areas as "Act I," "Act II," and so on. As in a play, each "act" presented something distinctive about the time, the place, the people, and their activities.

Four acts within the Wahpeton occupation area proved to be especially evocative: Act I showed signs of a lodge; Act II was a community dump; Act III had been a storage or resource processing area; and Act VI may have been a dance area. Act IV, near a possible fur trading post, added another dimension to the drama. Together, they provided vivid scenes of life at Little Rapids and inspired the events of the awl story.

Although images of the past first surfaced as we dug in each "act," the pictures became sharper in the lab as we cleaned, counted, identified, and analyzed the small, broken fragments of past lives. Some of these things implied what people did at Little Rapids; others suggested when they did it. While we found some evidence of settlement at Little Rapids before Europeans arrived in the area—particularly in the excavations nearest to the mounds—most of the things we retrieved dated to the nineteenth century. They appeared to be the remnants of a site occupied by one community for several summers, rather than a series of occupations by different groups separated by long periods of time. The archaeological record confirms written reports of a Wahpeton community based at Little Rapids for a time between the early and middle years of the century.

Included in the datable European- or American-made goods found in or near the major activity areas were gun parts, glass bottles and beads, metal hardware, buttons, and ceramic dishes (see CHART 2). Some of the beads, metal ornaments, and guns were manufactured specifically for the fur trade and would have been used by the Dakota residents of the site. Other items such as military buttons and European dishes might have originally belonged to Euro-American visitors or local fur traders. Since written records document distinctive design changes in these objects over a period of decades, they can be used to estimate the probable dates for the Wahpeton occupation. Though we do not know precisely how long it took European-manufactured goods to reach the Wahpetons through gift or trade, or how long people might have kept the goods before they were lost or discarded, their presence also indicates that the Wahpeton were at Little Rapids from about 1815 to 1850. Most of the datable objects in the assemblage clustered between the 1820s and 1840s. The sample of European ceramics found there suggests a likely occupation date, at least of the areas we excavated, as the late 1830s (FIGS. 36, 37).

SHADOWS OF A SUMMER LODGE (ACT I)
When we began our first field session, five teams of student excavators worked in randomly selected units scattered throughout the grid area. Each team encountered nineteenth-century materials in its square just a few centimeters underground, although some units produced more than others.

I assigned a sixth team to open up a square in another unit that differed markedly from the others. As the two novice excavators carefully removed the sod to expose an earlier living surface about ten centimeters beneath the present one, they came upon a thin layer of black, compacted, somewhat greasy-looking soil—a marked contrast to the sandy brown soils found at the same depth in the other squares.

Over two summer field seasons, crew members slowly opened up twenty-nine contiguous two-meter squares in this area, following the dark zone and searching for some delimiting border or boundary.

CHART 2.   Datable Artifacts

Datable fragments	Dates of manufacture
NEAR THE LODGE (ACT I)	
Essence-of-peppermint bottle	1820–60
Brass serpentine trade-musket side plate	1820–60
Military musket barrel tenon	1816
Military musket wedge plate	1816
Green faceted glass bead	After 1820
Polished white seed beads	1835–50
Tin-plated military trouser buttons	After 1850
IN THE DUMP (ACT II)	
Military musket sear spring	1816
Military musket gun sight	1816
Brass keyhole escutcheon	1830–37
U.S. Army greatcoat brass button	1820–39
Plain brass button	Before 1830
Red-striped white bead	After 1835
NEAR STORAGE AND PROCESSING AREA (ACT III)	
Percussion caps	After 1830
Flintlock hammer	1820–60
Pewter button	1815–21
Black faceted bead	After 1840
Amber wire-wound bead	After 1820
OTHER DATABLE ARTIFACTS	
Hudson's Bay bead (west of lodge)	1810–50
Red mold-blown faceted bead	
(north of lodge)	After 1845
ESTIMATED OCCUPATION DATES BASED ON SAMPLE OF EUROPEAN CERAMICS	
From sherds	1841
From estimate of total vessels	1839

SOURCES: Albert 1973; Eclov 1981; Hansen 1955; Jones 1981; Lofstrom 1976; Lofstrom personal communications 1981, 1988; Osman personal communication 1981; South 1978; Sprague n.d.; Withrow 1989

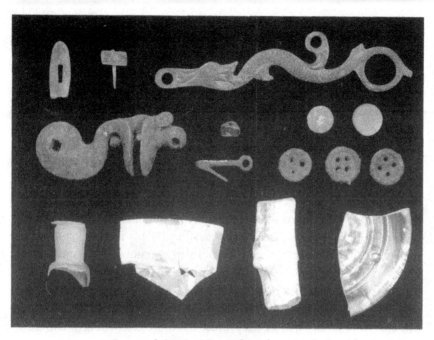

FIG. 36. Some of the datable artifacts from Little Rapids: (at top, from left) wedge plate, gun sight, serpentine trade-musket side plate; (middle) flintlock hammer, barrel tenon (above) and sear spring (below), buttons; (bottom) peppermint-bottle fragment, European ceramic sherds

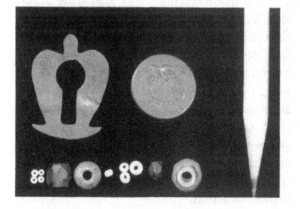

FIG. 37. Datable artifacts: (at top, from left) keyhole escutcheon, U.S. army greatcoat button; (bottom) four polished white seed beads, red mold-blown faceted bead, amber wire-wound bead, red-striped white seed bead, three polished white seed beads, green faceted bead, Hudson's Bay bead

In the process we encountered other distinctive features: thirteen large circles in the soil (FIGS. 38, 39). They looked like earth paintings, dappling the black background surface with subtle, lighter tones of dark browns and gray-browns. Five of them had an inner core of dark yellow or gray-brown soil surrounded by an outer circle of darker brown. All were circular or slightly oval in shape and about one meter in diameter.

As an archaeologist I knew these circles meant that Wahpeton people dug in this area before we did, although our purposes differed. They dug their holes to bury, hide, or preserve things; we dug ours to expose and retrieve things, gently scooping out the tinted soil that now filled the pits. We excavated half a circle at a time, following the original walls down to the pit floor, some almost a meter deep. In the artificial wall we created to divide the pit in two, we dug a small column and collected samples of earth at regular, five-centimeter intervals from top to bottom. We examined these in the lab, looking for remains too small to be seen while we were digging. After taking this sample, we removed the remaining soil, in the end re-creating the contours of the pits as they must have looked when Wahpeton people first dug them (FIG. 40).

The eleven pits we excavated completely appeared to be essentially empty. Whatever they once contained had perished or been removed. We encountered only a few things: in the bottom of one, a whole mussel shell; in others, fragments of broken bottle or window glass; sherds of European-made ceramics; tiny glass trade beads (probably manufactured in Venice, the source of most beads traded to North American Indians); an iron nail or two; flat, thin pieces of cut iron; small chips of pipestone and flint; a piece of an Indian-made tobacco pipe; a metal button and a small silver brooch; lead shot or residue from manufacturing shot; and a mainspring from a rifle made for the fur trade (APPENDIX 3). The pits also contained fragments of animal bone and pieces of charcoal. In one, we exposed a layer of ash and some white, powdery material that looked like disintegrating birch bark. After flotation testing and study of the residue left in the soil samples, we learned that all of the pits contained plant remains— mostly charred corn, berries, and nuts.

As we methodically traced the pattern of the black soil zone and circular pits, we uncovered other features: three small, irregularly shaped, shallow deposits of charcoal and ash—spots where small

FIG. 38. Overview of lodge area, looking southeast; note lighter soil areas marking storage pits near crew members.

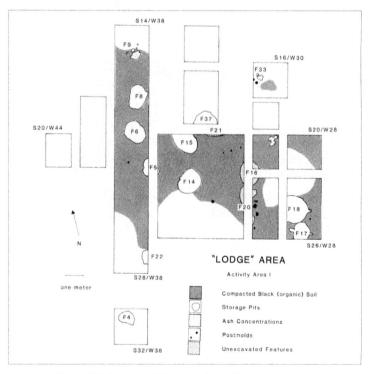

FIG. 39. Map of lodge area (Activity Area 1)

FIG. 40. Excavating and taking soil samples from storage pit in lodge area

fires had been built perhaps to smoke hides or control mosquitoes—and a pile of bones where someone had butchered part of a deer (APPENDIX 4A). We also found several scattered post molds where wooden poles forming the framework for scaffolds or buildings had rotted in the ground and left small, circular imprints.

After spending some weeks digging, we suspected that we were working in the vicinity of a lodge, a hub of community activity. We could envision how the earth became compacted and darkened by people trampling it while preparing food, eating meals, and making and repairing equipment and clothes. Our own activity produced a similar effect on the ground. It did not take long for the grass to flatten and die under our feet as we unintentionally smoothed the ground around our equipment tent and at the picnic tables where we took our breaks, wrote in our field journals, and ate lunch every day—and created a site for future archaeologists to study.

Nineteenth-century written records strengthened our sense of the activities associated with this part of the site. Samuel Pond reported that family members arrived at their summer villages after being separated for several months to collect maple sugar and trap muskrat.

These two activities could not be carried on by the same people at the same time "because the maple trees and muskrats were too far apart" (Pond [1908] 1986, 53).

As soon as the women returned to their planting villages, they began to repair their summer lodges or build new ones. Prescott said that the largest lodges or *tipi tonka*—twenty to thirty feet long and fifteen to twenty feet wide—could house four families, one living in each of the four corners (Black Thunder et al., 1975, 102; Prescott 1853, 236). Other lodges were smaller, depending on how many people lived there. Prescott also learned that lodges lasted seven or eight years with only minor repairs before needing to be replaced (Prescott 1854, 67). Many observers noticed as Pond did that "much of the labor of building was performed by women, but they were aided by the men who always put on the roof, that not being considered proper work for women" (Pond [1908] 1986, 38). The women's tasks included collecting the bark and wood needed for construction, clearing the ground, and erecting the buildings (see FIGS. 3, 31). A fascinated Pond described the process in considerable detail:

> In building them, they first set small posts in the ground, inclosing as large a space as the house was to occupy. These posts were set a foot or two apart, and were about three inches in diameter. On the sides of the house, they were five or six feet long reaching to the eaves, and on the gable ends they were longer toward the center, reaching to the roof. Strong forked posts were set at each end of the house, and, if necessary, one in the center, to support the ridgepole. The upper ends of the rafters rested on the ridgepole, and the lower ends on horizontal poles, which were fastened to the tops of the posts at the sides of the house. Small poles were placed transversely across the upright posts and the rafters, and were tied to the latter with basswood bark, so that the whole frame was a kind of wickerwork made of poles crossing each other at right angles. The covering of the house was taken from standing elm trees, a single bark being taken from each tree. The pieces of bark were five or six feet long and of different widths, according to the size of the trees from which they were taken. The bark was thick and some of the pieces were very heavy when green, being five or six feet square. They were fastened to the transverse pole with basswood bark, and the whole house was covered with them.

Those on the roof were lapped like shingles. The poles were all peeled, and the houses, when new, looked very neat. The doors were in the ends of the house, the larger houses having a door in each end, and the small ones having but one.

On each side of the interior of the house, running the whole length of it, and on three sides if there was but one door, a bench was constructed, about two feet high, covered with bark, and in some places spread over with buffalo robes and mats. These benches or bedsteads were five or six feet wide, and on them the inmates of the house sat, ate and slept (Pond [1908] 1986, 37–38).

The lodges were designed for summer living, well ventilated with sloping, waterproof roofs. Attached to them over the doors were scaffolds made of wooden poles. On hot nights people might sleep on the flat scaffold platform, while during the days it shaded people working underneath. Women also dried corn and skins on them (Densmore 1954, 16; M. Eastman 1853, 6).

Pond noticed another activity at the summer villages, which we discovered archaeologically: the Dakota constructed large bark barrels and placed them underground to hold corn not consumed immediately after harvesting. Although they ate some corn fresh, they preserved much of it by boiling it before it hardened. Then they scraped the kernels from the cob with a mussel shell or knife, dried it, and stored it in the underground barrels (Pond [1908] 1986, 27). "These barrels," Pond reported, "were made by bending broad pieces of bark around like hoops and lapping the ends together, sewing them with bark. The bottom was made of a circular piece of bark sewed on, and when the barrel was filled the top was covered in the same manner. These bark barrels held from two to five bushels. . . . They were neatly made, light and strong, and when kept dry were durable" (Pond [1908] 1986, 42).

Information from these nineteenth-century sources helped us plan our excavations. As we dug, we asked ourselves what might remain of the bark-covered lodges and underground storage barrels after more than a century of Minnesota rain, snow, freezes, and thaws. We felt fairly confident that the circular stains we had exposed represented the imprints of underground storage areas redefined by the passage of time. Although the pits were hidden from people passing the village after Dakota people left for the last time, burrowing rodents discovered them with little trouble and may have consumed the remaining contents. We could see their trails running through the soil filling the pits. Over time, the barrels collapsed and decomposed. The holes filled in with weather-driven debris, but their outlines still remained visible to us.

Although the Dakota concealed their underground storage areas, the women sometimes left behind other evidence of their work. We found a mussel shell that might have been someone's corn scraper and the remains of local plants and animals they harvested. Some plant and animal material might have been stored with the preserved corn, but it is more likely that the seeds and bone fragments had been washed into the pits from the surrounding work or living areas after the village had been abandoned.

The lodge proved more difficult to identify than the circular storage pits. Was the black soil zone we had exposed a time-frozen shadow of an earthen floor? Wahpeton people sometimes covered their lodge floors with perishable materials such as matting made of corn husks, reeds, or bulrushes (Black Thunder et al. 1975, 106). Corn husks would have been plentiful at Little Rapids; reeds and bulrushes filled the nearby marshes. We discovered seeds from plants of the sedge family (*Cyperaceae*) scattered throughout our soil samples from the storage pits and black soil zone (Shane 1982). Bulrushes (*Scirpus*) belong to this family, but, unfortunately, its species are not easily identified on the basis of seeds alone, the only evidence we found (Martin and Barkley 1961, 138).

Pond's description of an Eastern Dakota summer house is very specific about dimensions, shape, method of construction, and interior furnishings. Although we never discovered axes or hoes that women would have used to collect building materials for the lodges, amateur archaeologists digging at Little Rapids did. We should have been able to locate a central fireplace or trace post patterns outlining the rectangular lodge or the outdoor scaffolds, but we could not. Possibly the fireplace was in one of the two-meter squares we left unexcavated. Maybe the wooden wickerwork for the lodge walls was so secure that the posts could be rested on the ground surface instead of dug in, and they therefore did not decompose in place and stain the soil. Human scavengers undoubtedly took the long poles from the collapsing lodges soon after members of the Wahpeton community left Little Rapids for the last time. This removed traces of the lodge frame as well. The black, compacted dirt floor might be the only remaining remnant marking the place where a lodge once stood.

FIG. 41. Excavation at the dump; note ash lenses in foreground wall, animal bones at far left and scattered throughout area.

THE COMMUNITY DUMP (ACT II)

A week after identifying the possible lodge area, we started to investigate a place about forty meters to the southeast, on a slight rise. Evidence of diggers using metal detectors was conspicuous everywhere, and it did not take long to discover why. Our first two-meter square produced a larger array of materials than any of the others we had dug. As we continued opening up this area, eventually excavating eleven contiguous units, this pattern continued. Once outside the area, the number of artifacts and plant and animal remains declined dramatically.

Other notable features came to light here as well. Scattered on the ground from about ten centimeters to almost fifty centimeters below the surface were dozens of irregularly shaped, shallow deposits of gray ash (FIG. 41). Even in the field we could see that they contained charcoal, animal bones, and charred corn and nuts. Their size, shape, and composition suggested that people had cleaned out ash and other debris from their cooking-fire pits and dumped the remains here.

We found concentrations of other things in the dump, some visible in the field, others recognizable only after study in the lab: small clusters of charred plumstones, corn, and berries; a group of tiny white glass beads; pieces of cut sheet-iron, some made into decorative iron tinklers; several silver earrings, all of the same style and nestled together; and fragments of perforated iron sieves near some lead shot and the residue from manufacturing it.

Some of the things we found in the dump were unique or rare at the site, although they may have been more common when the Wahpeton lived there or before the collectors scavenged the site: an iron fishhook, one triangular iron arrow point, a bird-bone whistle, a wood-handled pocket knife, an ornamental keyhole plate, and the sear spring from a military musket. We also found four bone handles there, one complete—the focus of the awl story—and three fragmentary. One large fragment was unadorned, and the other two were inscribed with distinctive patterns. Day after day, we felt ourselves encountering the former residents of Little Rapids as directly as one can at an archaeological site.

We could imagine how this part of the site was created. It was not a place where people performed their daily activities but, rather, a place where they came after cleaning up their work areas. We could still see individual loads of waste material, things people had picked up after preparing and cooking meals, butchering muskrats or deer, cleaning fish, and making and repairing clothes, ornaments, and tools. Much of what we found was intentionally thrown away—worn out, broken, or otherwise unusable. But some objects such as the earrings and the glass beads seemed out of place here, perhaps inadvertently included with the garbage and other discarded material. While none of the nineteenth-century visitors to Dakota villages wrote about garbage-disposal practices, they described some of the activities that we found recorded so differently in the dump at Little Rapids. In combination, these two kinds of records helped us recreate the community.

Many of the things in the dump were remnants of Dakota women's lives. Two iron awl tips, the bone awl handles, one knife, and some of the animal bones attest to women's hide-working tasks, although these responsibilities would have taken much more attention and time than such meager remains suggest. Observers like Pond, Prescott, and the Eastmans recognized the importance of Dakota women's hide-working skills, but they did not know or think it important that the women's accomplishments were publicly recognized on their hide-working implements.

Dakota people in the 1830s still used skins, especially deer, for a variety of purposes. Although men sometimes butchered animals at the site of the kill, hide working was primarily women's work. Given the Dakota's reliance on animal hides and skins, curing them properly was an essential if time-consuming activity. Philander Prescott provided a detailed account of Eastern Dakota hide-working techniques. According to Prescott, women first removed an animal's skin and took off the flesh with a sharp bone tool.

> Then small holes are cut all round the skin; strings run all round, which are lashed to the poles of the lodge inside; the fire dries it in one night. . . . When they dress them, they take the grease off . . . then dip them into water wherein are brains of deer; boil and stretch them on four square poles tied, and pushed into the ground. They then commence scraping with a scraper made either of bone, horn, or iron. A fire is kept up to dry slowly. The women scrape until dry; then dip the skin in the brain-water, and scrape dry again; then dip in the water a third time. . . . [Smoking] is done by digging a hole in the ground about a foot deep, putting in a little fire and some rotten wood, when the skin is sewed into a bag and hung over the smoke: in ten minutes the skin is ready for use (Prescott 1854, 60–61).

Once the skins were prepared, they were made into tipi coverings, moccasins, shirts, leggings, garters, dresses, leather bags, cases, and other accessories. Women often decorated them with glass beads, quills, bells, and metal tinkling cones. These small ornaments were more easily broken or lost than the tools used to work the hides. We uncovered some of the ornaments near the lodge where the women did their beadwork, but many others found their way into the community dump where they appeared in far greater numbers than most other artifacts (APPENDIX 2).

Twentieth-century Wahpeton people recall that their ancestors created floral patterns in their beadwork, which they combined with images of butterflies, bluebirds, and deer (Black Thunder et al. 1975, 106). We recovered several hundred glass beads in the dump—mostly white, dark red, turquoise, and blue in color—but the patterns they might have formed were obliterated by the passage of time.

The tinkling cones we discovered—some iron and a few brass— were in various stages of completion. Some were finished, others only small, flat pieces of metal cut from old kettles, the "blanks" from which the cones were made. Dakota leatherwork now in museum and private collections shows these cones to have been popular decorations on buckskin dresses, moccasins, belts, bags, sashes, and cases of various sorts. When worn, "the rows of . . . cones added music as the wearer walked" (Markoe 1986, 105). A similar tinkling effect came from small brass bells attached to many articles. Along with glass beads, these bells commonly appeared on inventories of goods exchanged for furs at Little Rapids. We found several bells in the dump and others near the lodge where women probably worked with or wore them.

Dakota-made objects preserved in museum collections also illustrate how women combined brass tacks like the ones we discovered with beads, bells, and tinkling cones. Women also used furs, feathers, and porcupine quills for decoration, but these perishable materials no longer remained at the site. The bone fragments found in the dump—raccoon, woodchuck, flying squirrel, badger, river otter, grouse, woodpecker, and hawk—suggest that the residents might have hunted small animals and birds for ornamental furs and feathers (Whelan 1987; APPENDIX 4B). The total absence of porcupine remains at Little Rapids perplexes us, since quills were prominent in Dakota decorative work (Prescott 1854, 69; Pond [1908] 1986, 31–37). Although quills might have decayed, porcupine bones should have been preserved if the animals had been butchered at the site.

Mixed in the dump with the objects used to decorate clothing and other leather goods were personal ornaments. Like the other fur trade goods we found, these also were common items on the Little Rapids trading post inventories. They caught the eye of nineteenth-century observers such as Pond as well: "Besides the embroidery work of ribbons and beads with which they [the women] profusely decorated many of their garments, they wore other ornaments, some of which were of silver or imitation silver, among which were thin, circular plates, two or three inches in diameter, worn on the bosom, often many at once, so that the breast was nearly covered with them. The necks of many of the young women were loaded with beads, and their ears with earrings. . . . One girl wore seven pounds of beads on her neck at once" (Pond [1908] 1986, 33).

Some of the beads we uncovered in the dump were undoubtedly parts of necklaces. So were the small silver and brass jewelry links. We also found two brass finger rings, two brass buttons, and nine circular

FIG. 42. Earbobs found at Little Rapids

silver brooches. Finally, there were eight trade-silver "dangle" earrings, made for pierced ears (FIG. 42) and identical to the type shown
in Eastman's depiction of women harvesting wild rice (see FIG. 24).

In addition to signs of women's hide work, clothing, and ornamen-
tation, traces of other women's activities appeared in the dump. After
the women prepared plant and animal resources near their lodges, they
periodically brought waste materials there. Most of this refuse was the

remains of food left after roasting, boiling, drying, and consumption. For these processing activities, according to Euro-Americans who witnessed them, Dakota people used tin-plate, sheet-iron, copper, or brass containers and a variety of metal, bone, and wooden utensils and dishes (Prescott 1854, 67). Although containers and utensils made of animal bone and wood would not have survived years in the ground, metal ones would have. Yet the Dakota apparently did not break or throw away many metal utensils and containers, perhaps because they were considered valuable or could be reworked for another purpose. We rarely encountered them in the dump or anywhere else at the site, nor did the amateur collectors (APPENDIX 2).

Plant and animal remains were scattered widely throughout the dump, often mixed with ashes from the fire pits that we never found near the lodge and storage areas. One of the most common plant remains in the dump was corn. But burned cobs and kernel fragments only hint at the importance of the women's tasks associated with this single resource. The iron hoes exchanged by Dakota people for furs and later removed from the site by collectors provide an equally strong reminder of the women's horticultural responsibilities.

Mary Eastman was impressed that among the Dakota only women "plant, cultivate, and gather their corn, men rarely assuming any trouble with this" (M. Eastman 1853, 48). For women, community life from June through August focused on corn. The centrality of corn is further emphasized in the Dakota names for the months spent in the planting villages: "the Moon for Planting," "the Moon When Corn Is Hoed," and "the Moon When Corn Is Gathered" (Prescott 1852, 177).

The people who formed the Inyan Ceyaka Atonwan community during the summer would have regrouped there when wild strawberries began to ripen on the prairie. The ripening signalled that it was time to soak seed corn until it sprouted and was ready for planting. Then, according to Pond, women planted it "with their hands quite deep" in places where there was a "thrifty growth of wild artichokes, as they were likely to find the soil in such places rich and mellow" (Pond [1908] 1986, 27). At Little Rapids the fields were probably near the slough in the fertile, damp thickets (Fernald 1970, 1493; USFWS 1982, 5-10).

An account of planting corn appears in one of the Eastern Dakota stories collected in the late 1880s by Marie L. McLaughlin. Part Dakota and married to a Dakota Indian agent, McLaughlin heard the stories from older men and women living on the Devils Lake and Standing

Rock reservations (now in North and South Dakota). She wrote that before a woman "plants the first hill, she extends her hoe heavenwards and asks the Great Spirit to bless her work, that she may have a good yield. After her prayer she takes four kernels and plants one at the north, one at the south, one at the east and one at the west sides of the first hill. This is asking the Great Spirit to give summer rain and sunshine to bring forth a good crop" (McLaughlin [1916] 1990, 64).

Although we found places at Little Rapids where women stored their corn and discarded the unusable remains, we never located their cornfields. If they were near the slough, repeated flooding would have obliterated all signs of them. Pond, however, gave us a sense of how they might have looked:

> All the ground planted by them was dug up by the women with hoes. . . . They began by digging up a little conical mound for one hill, and then another by it, and so on, without any regular rows, till the little patch was dug over. . . . As soon as it showed three or four leaves, they loosened the earth around it with their fingers, and when it was large enough hilled it up thoroughly with hoes. They usually planted a small kind of corn that ripened early, but they had larger kinds and often raised good crops (Pond [1908] 1986, 27).

As the corn ripened, some of the women and children undoubtedly spent their days on scaffolds scaring blackbirds away from the corn. In a description accompanying Seth Eastman's engraving, *Guarding the Corn Fields* (for watercolor version, see FIG. 10), Mary Eastman wrote that

> the mode of scaring them off is an ingenious one. A scaffold, six or seven feet high, is raised in the field, and there the women and children sit, watching through the long day. Old women, or those who are feeble and cannot otherwise employ themselves, generally perform this part. Children are glad to be called upon; for while they sit under the robe which forms a kind of awning, they can dance, or talk and laugh, or what is still better, listen to long, miraculous stories about beavers or bears . . . or about great black spiders that have journeyed all over the world (M. Eastman 1853, 48).

Visitors to Little Rapids in the 1830s also might have seen women going out from the village to collect wild vegetables, nuts, and fruits for foods, beverages, medicines, and dyes. The marshy areas surrounding the site provided aquatic grasses and vegetables. The lowland and upland forests and thickets offered other key resources. Elm, oak, maple, red cedar, box elder, hackberry, and basswood trees produced wood and bark for construction, fuel, and manufacture of containers, tools, and utensils. Nuts and saps provided food. The forests and thickets also supplied berries that women used in foods, medicines, beverages, and dyes and served as home to the large and small animals that provided meat, fat, hides, bones, sinew, and furs.

In the Inyan Ceyaka Atonwan dump and storage pits near the lodge area, we discovered some residues of wild plant resources along with the corn. We know from the charred seeds and nutshells found in our soil samples that the Wahpeton gathered hazelnuts, wild raspberries, grapes, elderberries, strawberries, cherries, and plums from the thickets and forests near the village (Shane 1984). Dakota women reportedly also used plums in one of their games of chance, which utilized "plum-stones which had certain marks burnt upon them. The plum-stones were a kind of dice, and after they had been shaken up in a wooden dish, the latter was set down suddenly so that the jar caused them to rebound" (Pond [1908] 1986, 118; Prescott 1854, 64). The plum pits from Little Rapids, however, even under magnification, showed no burn marks.

Our list of plants recovered from the dump resembles those named by Pond and Prescott. Although our inventory proved more extensive than theirs (APPENDIX 5), they mentioned several important wild plant foods that must have been available locally but, like other marsh and prairie root crops, did not survive as archaeological remains. Little Rapids women must have collected root plants like *psincha, psinchincha,* and water lilies in the slough or nearby marshes and shallow lakes, for these were reportedly staples of their summer diet (Pond [1908] 1986, 28). The women probably searched the dry upland prairies for wild turnips, the potato-like root called *mdo,* and a starchy, turnip-like plant known as *teepsinna* (Riggs 1869, 17; Woolworth and Woolworth 1977, 86–88).

We found only scant evidence in the dump of the resources that Dakota women reportedly collected for dyes: sumac berries used to make red dye and a few small lumps of red ochre, or iron oxide, valued for its reddish-brown color. This was probably just a small sample of what they used. According to Prescott, "They dye red, purple, blue, black, green, yellow. The red dye is made from the top of the sumach and a small root found in the ground, by boiling. Yellow is from flowers by boiling. Black is from maple-bark, butternut, and black mud taken from the bottom of rivers. . . . Oxide of iron is found, and makes paint very much like Spanish brown, and is much used by all" (Prescott 1854, 69).

Some of these colors held important symbolic meaning for the Wahpeton. According to Black Thunder,

> Black represents the west where the powers of the thunderbird exist whose job it is to make rain and keep rivers, lakes and streams from being defiled. White represents the north where the Waziya [god of the north] lives whose powers are to provide strong cleansing winds and to put Mother Earth to rest by giving a snow cover for shelter. In this way Mother Earth regains her power to produce more living things. Red represents the east where the sun rises giving all knowledge, wisdom, and understanding. Yellow represents the south where the power from the south winds creates souls of men and to where the souls return (Black Thunder et al. 1975, 116).

The contents of the Little Rapids dump reinforced nineteenth-century observations that women did most of the subsistence and manufacturing work in Dakota summer communities. But the dump also held materials associated with men. Fish and turtle, consumed in "great quantities," were the most commonly occurring animal remains in the dump, and both men and women fished and captured turtles (Pond [1908] 1986, 30). Women cooked large fish by roasting or boiling them whole (Prescott 1854, 67). The uncharred remains of drumfish, the most abundant fish at Little Rapids, indicate that they were cooked by boiling. Then the meat was removed and the carcasses carried to the dump. In one excavated square, we uncovered a pile of fish bones that later analysis showed were the remains of at least twenty-one individual drumfish, all about seventeen inches long and weighing about three pounds (Whelan 1987, 131, 140, 145). These bottom-dwelling fish would have been plentiful in the Minnesota River in early summer and could have been caught easily with nets as the fish spawned in shallow waters near shore.

The Dakota also prepared turtles by boiling (Riggs 1869, 25). A comparison of the pattern of turtle remains in the dump to the turtle remains in the lodge area indicates things about their preparation and use not mentioned in the documentary records. Though Little Rapids residents captured five different species of turtle, the most common were the painted turtle and the snapping turtle. From the distribution of bones and shells, it appears that they were used for different purposes. Both the shells and the skeletal parts of the snapping turtle's meatier body were in the dump, suggesting that this species was butchered primarily for meat. In contrast, the only painted-turtle remains that we discovered were shells, hinting that the Dakota did not eat painted-turtle meat but instead used their shells for dishes, utensils, or rattles (Whelan 1987, 112–20).

According to nineteenth-century reports, Dakota men hunted and trapped a variety of other animals depending on the season. Deer, ducks, and geese provided the most important summer animal resources, but the men also killed birds and a few elk and bear. Muskrat, skunk, ermine, mink, raccoon, rabbit, otter, beaver, and fisher (a carnivorous, weasel-like mammal) were sought for their pelts, which the Indians traded for goods or manufactured into bags and other articles (Pond [1908] 1986, 29; Prescott 1854, 60).

Like the plant remains, the animal remains in the dump reinforced impressions gleaned from contemporary written sources and, again, yielded more specifics. Animal bones were found scattered throughout the site, but the vast majority of them must have been taken to the dump as waste after butchering, cooking, processing, and eating. Drumfish, muskrat, deer, and snapping and painted turtle dominated the animal assemblage. In all, we discovered five turtle, nine fish, twenty-one bird (mostly waterfowl), and thirteen mammal species (Whelan 1987; APPENDIX 4B). When combined with corn and wild plant foods, the animal remains suggest the existence of a relatively diverse diet during the summer months of the 1830s—hardly the "poor and miserable" fare that Agent Taliaferro described in his 1839 report on the Wahpeton.

Just as we found few tools associated with women's activities in our excavations, we discovered few traces of men's hunting, trapping, or fishing equipment. By the early nineteenth century, these goods would have been acquired by the Wahpeton through fur traders. An 1827 invoice of goods delivered to François La Bathe for trade at Little Rapids, for example, included fifteen northwest guns, five kegs of powder, two pounds of shot, three hundred flints, more than three hundred pounds of lead, sixty-six muskrat traps, thirteen muskrat spears, forty-five beaver traps, and eight dozen knives (La Bathe 1828).

Although animal remains provide information about hunting, fishing, and trapping, our artifact sample does not accurately represent the material goods associated with these activities. In part this is because we were preceded at Little Rapids by several generations of artifact collectors. We recovered only one trap part, one fishhook, and one metal projectile point from the dump, one trap part near the lodge, and twenty-five small metal gun parts from the rest of the site (five of which were found in the dump). In contrast, three artifact collectors who combed the site before us discovered remains of at least nineteen guns, twenty-two knives, twenty-one fishhooks, twenty-two iron projectile points, twenty-three muskrat spears, and eight trap parts (see APPENDIX 2).

For our efforts, we found some smaller remnants of men's activities, including gunflints, musket balls, buckshot, and shot, but we discovered much more evidence of the manufacture of ammunition from lead bars provided by fur traders. Pond reported that the Wahpeton produced lead shot "by pouring it through a sieve of perforated bark held over water, the sieve being jarred while the lead was running, so that it fell into the water in drops" (Pond [1908] 1986, 40). Broken sieves surfaced in the dump—a dozen pieces of perforated sheet metal, which would have replaced or supplemented the old bark sieves. The size of the holes in the sieves varied according to the desired size of the shot (FIG. 43). We also found hundreds of pieces of lead residue left behind as a by-product of the manufacturing process.

The final clue that we uncovered of the men at Little Rapids was small but unmistakable: fragments of pipestone. Pond reported the presence of pipestone among the Dakota, noting that during the summer, "some of the men went to the red pipestone quarry [now *Pipestone National Monument*] and brought home pieces of the stone for pipes." They quarried the southwestern Minnesota stone with hoes and axes and, using their knives, made beautiful small pipe bowls. The stems, said Pond, "which were two or three feet long, were made of young ash trees, the pith being bored out with a wire." Dakota men spent

FIG. 43. Gun parts, ammunition, and flints from Little Rapids, photographed with an illustration of a trade musket

a good deal of time fashioning and ornamenting pipes and used them often (Pond [1908] 1986, 58, 123; Prescott 1852, 176).

Pipes made of this cherished red stone still play an important role among the Dakota. This attachment was brought to life for us when Dakota spiritual leader Amos Owen conducted a pipe ceremony at Little Rapids and passed his sacred pipe around our circle. According to one modern commentator,

> Pipes were—and continue to be—the means by which the people communicate with the spirit world. Traditionally, the pipe was smoked to bring a spiritual dimension to human affairs, to seal an agreement, to bind the smokers to a common task . . . or to signal a willingness to discuss an issue. As the smoke rises upward, it carries the prayers of the smoker. This is why a pipe smoker will always offer the pipe to the four sacred directions before smoking (Sletto 1992, 24).

We found evidence of pipe making near the lodge, where the men must have done this work, and in the dump, where they discarded broken and unfinished pieces and the flakes from their carvings. In all, we recovered seventeen pipe-bowl fragments, as well as other pipestone objects. We discovered a small, flat, circular disk, perhaps part of a pendant or other ornament, ten worked pieces of the stone, and seventy-eight pipestone flakes. More of the finished pieces were found near the lodge, while most of the manufacturing debris was retrieved in the dump. Looking back, we see that the excavations at Act I, the lodge area, and Act II, the community dump, told us more about some specifics of Wahpeton daily life and activities than our key nineteenth-century observers thought to convey or, perhaps, ever knew. In contrast our digging at Acts VI and IV left us as troubled as we were enlightened.

EIGHT

GLIMPSES OF COMMUNITY LIFE

Part II

Two areas of the site, Act VI and Act IV, were elusive and disturbing, although for different reasons. In both, the past and the present collided in ways we did not foresee. The clues to the past were tantalizing, the ethics of digging exposed.

RETRACING STEPS TO A POSSIBLE DANCE AREA (ACT VI)
When Theodore Lewis first found Little Rapids in August 1887, he observed a low earthen embankment forming an oval-shaped enclosure just north of the group of mounds (see FIG. 20). He described these features in the terse style typical of that period:

> This group numbers 29 tumuli. Besides the embankment making the enclosure, which is generally about 12 ft. wide, there are six elongated mounds which are from 22 ft. to 24 ft. wide. Nos. 6 and 7 are at least partly composed of stone. One mound, No. 29, is flat-topped, the top being 28 ft. in diameter and the bottom 50 ft., [and] 3 ft. high. The ends of the enclosure overlap 28 ft. The width of the embankment varies from 8 ft. to 13 ft. Surveyed Aug. 24, 1887 (Winchell 1911, 191).

Features such as this were not unique to Little Rapids; just three weeks earlier, Lewis had mapped similar, somewhat larger enclosures northwest of Little Rapids near Clearwater Lake and Clearwater River in Wright County (Winchell 1911, 217, 219). He had observed other earthen embankments throughout the state, but most were straight, rather than curved to form enclosures. Although there was speculation about the purpose of these features—Lewis would probably have attributed them to the ancient mound-builders, while others suggested that the Indians had built them for defense—early archaeologists remained uncertain about how, when, or why the enclosures had been constructed (Winchell 1911, 407–08).

If Lewis had visited Dakota villages several decades earlier, he might have observed features that resembled the earthen enclosures. Pond's and Seth Eastman's descriptions of Dakota dance areas noted two distinctive characteristics: an oval shape and a low fence or barrier separating the audience from the participants (see FIG. 9). Pond chronicled the construction and appearance of Dakota dance areas in considerable detail:

> A smooth, dry place was selected and inclosed by setting stakes around it four or five feet in height, and tents were then hung on the poles or stakes. The inclosure was eight or ten rods long and twenty or thirty feet wide, and the fence so low that the spectators could look over it. At one end of the inclosed space a large shelter was constructed by putting several tents together, so arranged that the side toward the dancing-ground was always open during the dance. This tent was the headquarters of the principal men and women, for the lodge was composed of both sexes in about equal numbers. . . .
>
> When the day for the dance arrived, a number of large kettles, filled with choice food, were hung over a fire at the end of the enclosure, opposite the tent, and persons were appointed to attend them during the day (Pond [1908] 1986, 94).

Anthropologist Alanson B. Skinner, who learned about the medicine dance in the early twentieth century from Wahpeton elders living near Sisseton, South Dakota, described dance enclosures similarly. He reported that the enclosures were aligned east to west with a single, open entrance at the east end where feasts were cooked for performers. An open tent formed the west end of the enclosure (Skinner 1920, 272–73). Eastman's illustrations of the medicine dance closely conform to Pond's and Skinner's descriptions.

When we began excavating at Little Rapids in 1980, we knew about the oval enclosure from the maps drawn by Lewis and, more than sixty years later, by the Klammers. Collectors had used the maps to guide their probings, and when three of them accompanied us to the site, they reported finding fur trade goods in the area. Pursuing these leads, we excavated a single two-meter square in the vicinity of the enclosure. When we found little evidence of nineteenth-century activity, we turned elsewhere and did not return until 1986. Randall M. Withrow, the field supervisor that year, was particularly interested in earthworks, and he and several crew members devised a plan to locate the embankment again.

This proved to be a challenge, because sumac had completely covered the area and obscured the ground surface. But we were curious to know if the enclosure still existed and if it was linked to the 1830s Wahpeton community that we knew a good deal more about than we had in 1980.

With a copy of Lewis's map and field notes in hand, Randy and several others tried to retrace Lewis's steps of a century earlier. Using a compass and measuring tapes, they placed small markers on the ground or on sumac branches to outline where the embankment should be if it had survived. By the next day, when the crew had cleared off enough sumac to see the ground, parts of the embankment emerged just as Lewis had shown it. After another day of clearing brush, the entire area became visible (FIG. 44), and with the exception of some amateur digging and our small 1980 test square, much of the large enclosure remained in excellent condition.

Though some portions were more prominent than others, we could now see the low embankment, about a foot in height, and the irregular oval-shaped area it enclosed. Oriented from east to west, the enclosure was some thirty-five meters long and twenty-two meters wide (Withrow 1989c, 2).

Our Dakota colleague Chris Cavender was unfamiliar with nineteenth-century Dakota dance areas. He had a great deal of experience with modern Dakota powwows, however, and he did not see much similarity between the dance areas in Eastman's illustrations and those used by contemporary Dakota. Together we began studying the documentary descriptions more carefully to determine whether this area might have been the site of Wahpeton dances and related activities.

FIG. 44. Locating the possible dance area (Activity Area VI)

We did not need to do much excavating to determine that this enclosure was linked to the nineteenth-century Wahpeton community. In the two narrow trenches we excavated through the embankment, one on the west side and another on the north, we found materials very similar to those in the community dump: animal bone fragments, charcoal, ash, glass trade beads, metal fragments, and pieces of nineteenth-century ceramics. In contrast to the relatively dense concentration of materials in the embankment, we found very little in the five small, square pits we then excavated inside the enclosure.

It seemed to us that people had cleaned the flat area now within the boundaries of the enclosure and, in the process, created a low earthen wall of refuse composed of the topsoil and accumulated refuse. Pond mentions that Dakota women cleared and leveled the ground surface with hoes before constructing their lodges (Pond [1908] 1986, 39, 46). Perhaps, in much the same way, they periodically cleared the surface before holding a dance. The slight rise this created may have been the foundation for the hide-covered wooden framework that, as Eastman illustrated, created a low barrier between the dancers and the audience.

    With little time left for excavations that season we were unable
to confirm our tentative identification of a dance area. More extensive digging might have revealed traces of an open dancers' tent at
the west end of the enclosure or cooking fires at the opposite end.
Additional excavation might also have yielded some remnants of the
paraphernalia that Skinner reported was associated with the medicine
dance, such as water drums, gourd rattles, and medicine bags made
from the skins of otters, white muskrats (used only by men), certain
kinds of ducks, and prairie dogs. Other items included root and herbal
medicines, special quills and feather plumes, and wooden bowls and
spoons used for feasting, the latter with distinctive handles carved to
represent animals. Also important were records of songs to be sung,
made by carving symbolic figures on small pieces of flat board (Skinner
1920, 264–68). Dancers undoubtedly would have treated such valuable
materials with special care, and the objects probably would not have
entered the archaeological record by being lost, broken, or abandoned.
Even if they had been lost or left behind, most would have decayed
beyond recognition.

    We found, however, one set of materials that Skinner mentioned
as associated with the medicine dance: "Members wore necklaces of
cowrie shells and bone beads, both of which were supposed to be alive.
Thimbles were attached to these necklaces, in which dried fireflies
were placed, the idea being that whenever such a necklace was worn,
no one would be angry with the wearer" (Skinner 1920, 267). Our
excavations uncovered one cowrie shell, one carved bone bead, and
one ornamental thimble with cuts and perforations (FIG. 45). Although
they were not found together or even near the dance area, these one-
of-a-kind clues proved tantalizing. The fact that Mazomani was a well-
known leader of the medicine lodge strongly suggests that the dance
would have been held at Little Rapids.

    In 1988 Randy Withrow considered doing more extensive field
testing near the enclosure to see if any conclusive evidence might surface. Prior to digging, he consulted with members of the Minnesota
Indian Affairs Council. Although our Dakota colleagues had not done
so when we worked together at Little Rapids, some council members
strongly objected to any excavation there. To them, a dance area—
even a suspected one—was sacred and, like a burial place, should not
be disturbed. Respecting their views, Randy did not dig further in
the enclosure or embankment.

FIG. 45. Cowry shell, carved bone bead, and thimble from possible dance area

This episode of the Little Rapids drama was a humbling reminder of the ethical dilemmas of practicing archaeology. None of us intended to be disrespectful or insensitive in pursuing our hunch that members of the Little Rapids community might have danced within the enclosure. In fact, we will never know for certain that this feature of the landscape or the pieces of necklace found nearby were associated with the medicine dance. Still, the archaeological clues, combined with Eastman's illustrations and Pond's and Skinner's accounts, elicted images of life at Little Rapids that we would have missed otherwise. Do I wish we might have had a chance to follow these tantalizing leads? Yes. Would I knowingly dig in sacred areas? No.

TROUBLING SIGNS OF THE LITTLE RAPIDS TRADING POST (ACT IV)

The last activity area we explored at Little Rapids raised yet another set of archaeological dilemmas—this time provoked by the destructive work of amateur archaeologists. Just north of Johnson's Slough, some two hundred meters north of the Wahpeton encampment, lay one of the most intriguing and frustrating activity areas at Little Rapids. One artifact collector believed that the flat peninsula of high ground overlooking Johnson's Slough and the surrounding marsh had been

CHART 3.   Fur Traders at Little Rapids

Jean Baptiste Faribault (J.B.F.)	1802–8, 1827, 1829–37
Alexander Faribault (son of J.B.F.)	1828, and with J.B.F.
Oliver Faribault (son of J.B.F.)	With J.B.F. and Alexander, 1836–47
Luther Lamont	1825–26
Francis Grandin	1822–23, 1826
François La Bathe	1822–23, 1826–29
Louis Provençalle	1826
Charles Brush	1828–29
James Wells	1834–36
Duncan Cameron	1836
Louis Robert	1850–51

SOURCES: MHS n.d

the site of Faribault's busy trading post. Other men had also been licensed by the American Fur Company (see CHART 3) to trade somewhere in this vicinity between 1802 and 1851.

During the 1980 field season we had excavated a series of one-meter-square test pits between the Wahpeton encampment and the possible trading post. Most of these pits proved archaeologically sterile, but as we neared the possible site of the former post, signs of nineteenth-century activity increased. At the end of our 1981 field season, two crew members tested the area more intensively, looking for any artifacts that would connect it to the Wahpeton community. Based on the remains discovered, we had estimated the date of Wahpeton occupation to be the 1830s and 1840s. If the supposed fur post site were related, test excavations should reveal some chronological overlap.

After spending the morning working in the area of the post, the two crew members joined the rest of us for lunch. In their excavation of a one-meter-square test pit about 218 meters north and 238 meters west of where we were working, they had found objects from the ground surface down through twenty centimeters. Then they opened their artifact bag to show us what they had discovered. Among other things, they had unearthed an incredible time link between the two Little Rapids sites. In the second excavation level of their unit, about fifteen centimeters deep, they had found an 1841 dime in perfect condition (FIG. 46). With it at the same depth were materials dating from

FIG. 46. Dime, dated 1841, found in possible post area

FIG. 47. Overview of possible post area (Activity Area IV)

the same period, including a white clay or kaolin pipestem, fragments of iron, broken window glass, and square nails. Although the coin theoretically could have been lost long after its minting date, the accompanying fragments suggest that this would have been unlikely. All signs suggested a trading post contemporary in time with the village site. Accordingly, I decided to focus our fieldwork on that promising part of Little Rapids.

During the summer of 1982 we spent six weeks excavating the post area but with frustrating results (FIG. 47). We found a wealth of archaeological materials—literally thousands of artifacts, building materials, and plant and animal remains representing centuries of human activity. Fragments of stone tools and indigenous ceramics indicated that Indians had occupied the area long before Euro-American colonization. Glass beads and trade-silver ornaments signalled activity during the fur trade. But mixed in with these memory traces were many more artifacts from other time periods.

In fact, it was impossible to determine if a fur post had stood on the site because digging by amateur archaeologists and collectors over the years had damaged the entire area beyond usefulness. Some evidence suggested activity contemporary with the Wahpeton community, but in most excavation units, from the surface on down, remains from the early and mid-nineteenth century were mixed with precontact Indian artifacts and materials from the late nineteenth and early twentieth centuries. In addition, we found soda cans, cigarette filters, tin foil, sherds of plastic cups, brown beer-bottle glass, and bottle caps—signs of a late twentieth-century site thoughtlessly created by an amateur archaeologist.

Time-jumbling digging by collectors had shattered the boundaries of time and culture to produce an archaeological nightmare. An uncritical reading of the evidence found in the ground could easily produce this impossible scenario:

An elderly woman and man—perhaps distant relatives of the Wahpeton who lived at Little Rapids in the 1800s—sat together on a large flat rock overlooking the peaceful slough below. Taking a brief break from their work, they smoked cigarettes and shared a soda.

As a white egret gracefully landed on the water to feed, the woman put out her cigarette, took a last sip of the soda, and threw the can away. Her husband picked up the small, white stone point he was finishing and, using a bone flaking tool, he removed small flakes along the edges and base to create a perfectly shaped triangle. Meanwhile, she resumed working on the clay pot she was making to replace a broken one, carefully adding grit to the clay to prevent it from cracking.

A short distance away, a fur trader lit his white clay pipe, opened a bottle of beer, and emptied it into his plastic cup. He watched the man and woman work, perplexed. Why did she still prefer her handmade pots to the brass and iron kettles he kept in stock? Why did the man continue to manufacture stone points, when, in exchange for a few furs, he could have had iron ones to haft onto the shafts of arrows?

Our frustration in trying to make sense of a mix of unrelated material remains and false associations was acute. Despite extensive testing, we could not discern any traces of a structure where nineteenth-century fur traders might have lived or stored their goods. There was no way to tell if the trade materials we found there belonged to Indians who lived nearby or were the remaining stock of a trader who hoped to exchange the items for furs. Our analysis of the thousands of artifacts recovered from this disturbed activity area remains incomplete, and we will probably never know what went on here in the 1830s and 1840s.

In some ways, however, this activity area tells its own poignant story. In one relatively small piece of land, we found traces of Little Rapids' earliest Indian occupants, its later Wahpeton residents, nineteenth-century fur traders, early American settlers, and late twentieth-century artifact collectors, all buried together in an odd crypt. It is a haunting archaeological metaphor: the present intruding into the past and the past embracing the present.

WHAT DOES
THIS ALL
MEAN?

C URRENT EVENTS SOMETIMES call up the past. In the fall of 1991 and winter of 1992, the Atlanta Braves and the Washington Redskins traveled to Minneapolis for the World Series and the Super Bowl, respectively. During the games these teams and their fans encountered real Indian people and their supporters who protested the appropriation of Indian names and symbols by sports teams. The protesters objected to the use of feathered headdresses, tomahawks, war paint, and chants as demeaning and racist. Addressing a crowd, Clyde Bellecourt, national director of the American Indian Movement, linked this disrespectful trivialization of Indian culture to a longer history of oppression. He observed, "They call us radicals and militants. . . . Only a few years ago, they were calling us savages and heathens." In response, a Super Bowl fan shouted back, "Why don't you go back to the reservation?" (Furst 1992).

Nationally and locally, cultural collisions between Indians and Euro-Americans have a long history. Non-Indian people have romanticized, ridiculed, and misrepresented Indian cultures to justify the seizure of land, the mistreatment of burial remains, the silences and offenses in classrooms and in the media, and the appropriation of Indian names for streets in neighborhoods. Perhaps if more non-Indian Americans knew what life was like for Indian people during and after the period of settlement by Euro-Americans, they would view Indians differently and, among other things, abandon the use of Indians as team mascots.

As producers of public knowledge about Indian histories and cultures, archaeologists and historians could play a positive role in breaking through these barriers to empathy. We cannot erase history, but we can rewrite it. This idea has guided me in presenting what we have learned about the Wahpeton community at Little Rapids.

My initial concern in this project had been to bring a feminist perspective to archaeology. To counteract the negative effects of the field's bias, I wanted to highlight the activities of women and the centrality of gender as a significant and dynamic factor shaping encounters between Dakota people and Euro-American settlers.

As the project unfolded and Dakota people joined it, I became increasingly aware of my privilege by race and by profession, especially as I wrote about the history and experiences of their nineteenth-century relatives at Inyan Ceyaka Atonwan. For too long, I could see, archaeological writings have perpetuated rather than counteracted pejorative Indian imagery.

Now as the project comes to a close, I wish I could have had the opportunity that researchers who work in contemporary settings do: to return to the people they study before a work is published and discuss the way in which the people are portrayed (Mbilinyi 1989; Rosaldo 1989). These researchers can get feedback about how well or how poorly they grasped and communicated the essential qualities of the individuals' lives, actions, and feelings. In turn, this input can contribute to the final fashioning of a paper, book, film, or other presentation.

Collaborations of this kind are impossible for archaeologists. The closest I have come is presenting my work to some of Mazomani's descendants. After hearing me tell the awl story accompanied by slides of the Little Rapids site and dig, Chris Cavender asked me to present the slide lecture to his mother and her eldest son, Caske (Harry C. Crooks). When I did, they seemed to appreciate the work, although they did not say much. Elsie spoke a bit about her grandmother, Mazaokiyewin, remembering her reputation for beautiful leather work and beadwork. Caske said something like: "That work at Little Rapids, it was a good thing." Later Chris told me that they especially liked the narrative because it featured Mazaokiyewin.

More recently, I was invited to speak about Little Rapids to a group of volunteer interpreters who guide public tours through the Minnesota Valley National Wildlife Refuge. Although I did not know that he would be there, Chris's cousin Gary Cavender, who had visited

Little Rapids with us, was in the audience. After the lecture, he spoke about his great-grandmother. The story of how the awl came to rest in the ground rekindled some memories of her.

Gary remembered Mazaokiyewin as elderly, the way she looked in Monroe Killy's photograph. He told us that as a little boy, he loved to lie on her lap while she rubbed his back, singing a song he later sang to his own children. It was a Dakota song warning children to be quiet because Ojibway enemies might be nearby. Gary laughed about singing this to his children because his wife was Ojibway. He also remembered his great-grandmother bringing him jelly beans. The volunteer interpreters had known little about the archaeology, the history, or the Wahpeton community at Little Rapids. Once again, a member of Mazomani's family provided a link between the past and the present.

I still find myself wishing for a time machine. I dream of spending just one day at Little Rapids with some members of our project—Chris Cavender, Ed Cushing, Sara Evans, Carrie Schommer, Diane Stolen, Mary Whelan, and Randy Withrow—and some of the nineteenth-century figures linked to Inyan Ceyaka Atonwan: Mazaokiyewin, Mazomani, Hazawin, Jean B. Faribault, and Stephen Riggs. Instead of returning to the past, this encounter would take place in the present. I can visualize the day, but it is difficult to picture how we would communicate, given the distances between us.

It would be early morning and quiet as we walked along the trail to the site through the burial area. (I shudder at the thought of the people seeing the collectors' gaping intrusions into their ancestral mounds.) The day might begin, as our days so often did during the summer field schools, with a site tour. I would ask our nineteenth-century colleagues to lead the way and each of them to take us to places they found especially meaningful. Each person would un-doubtedly lead us in a different direction, telling us about different events, activities, people, and relationships. Then we would show them the places we found important. The Wahpeton people might tease us about our interest in their dump. Maybe if they saw some of the things that we found there—the inscribed awl handles, fragments of red-brown pipestone, glass beads, silver earrings, bells, and tinkling cones—they would understand why it became such a vibrant place for us. Would they be surprised that we had discovered these remarkable traces of their lives?

I wonder how the Wahpeton women would react to our finding the hidden places where they had stored their surplus corn. Would they show us where they had planted and protected it? Would they be willing to take us to their favorite spots for gathering berries, nuts, marsh plants, and the other resources available during the summer months? I imagine Diane and Randy heading off toward the oval enclosure with Mazomani. What would he tell them about it? Would Mazomani and Riggs speak to each other? Would Faribault confirm the collectors' beliefs about the location of his post? Would Hazawin and Mazomani ask Chris and Carrie about their family? About their losses? How would they feel about our digging in their community? Questions and images tumble through my mind. What could we really say to each other, connected as we are through this one place, yet coming from such different worlds?

APPENDIXES

APPENDIX I. Staff/Consultants and Field School Crews

Mary K. Whelan, anthropology graduate student, teaching/research assistant and lab supervisor, 1980–81

Randall M. Withrow, anthropology graduate student, teaching/research assistant, and lab supervisor, 1986–87

Nancy Buck, Lynne Dablow, Teresa Halloran, and Diane M. Stolen, undergraduate field-school students; teaching/research assistants and lab supervisors

Barbara H. O'Connell, professor of anthropology, Hamline University; staff member and supervisor of students, 1982

Edward J. Cushing, professor of ecology and behavioral biology, University of Minnesota; field ecologist, 1986

Sara M. Evans, professor of history, University of Minnesota; volunteer excavator, 1980; field-school ethnohistorian, 1986

Carolynn I. Schommer, Dakota language instructor, University of Minnesota; field-school language instructor, 1986

Chris C. Cavender, project consultant, 1985 to present; field-school Dakota history and culture instructor, 1986

Brent P. Olson, graduate student, University of Minnesota; field surveyor, 1986; researcher, 1986–87

Elizabeth M. Scott, graduate student, historical archaeology and zooarchaeology, University of Minnesota; honors-seminar teaching assistant, 1986–87; analyzed animal bones found in 1986

Linda Shane, research specialist, University of Minnesota; identified plant remains found in 1980–81

Edward U. Lofstrom, Stephen E. Osman, Jeffrey P. Tordoff, staff members, Minnesota Historical Society; identified and dated materials from Little Rapids

Christy A. H. Caine, Sara M. Evans, Barbara Presley Noble, Jan Streiff; helped test the site in 1979

Crews

1980: Sheri Alexander, Greg Baldwin, Patti Baldwin, Jan Curry, June Chase, Lynne Dablow, Mary Jaeger, Bill Johnston, June Junqueira, Sherrie Karch, Ken Koybayashi, Mary Ellen Kelly, Ted Leines, Mike McCrum, Howard Maxwell, Melissa Meyer, Mary Beth Reed, Millie Resch, Lisa Roche, Jeff Skoog, Gary Stammer, Toni Ziegler.

1981: Jane Anderson, Nancy Buck, Betsy Dablow, Sue Graak, Mary Greeman, Teresa Halloran, Linda Hill, Frank Holmgren, Jerry Kramer, John Mahoney, Noel Menard, Laurie Nelson, Scott Nelson, Teresa Puff, Ruth Raich, Bonnie Ryg, Gary Stammer, Mary Wright.

1982: Blythe Carlson, Felice Christenson, Lucretia Chamberlain, John Cardinal, Jim Dobrahner, Dawn Fleming, Jana Fortier, Glynis Gilbert, Lynette Goemer, Teresa Halloran, Ken Kramer, Jean Miller, Tom Miller, Cindy Moncrief, Marcia Regan, Jennifer Ross, Sharon Tibesar, Jeff Tolefson.

1986: Kerrie Blevins, Lisa Bromer, Margaret Craig, Vicki Griggs, Lia Hostetler, Jane Kientiz, Jill Mitchell, Anne Mobarry, Lucy Mueller, Monty Nelson, Reid Nelson, Scott Nemanic, Amelia Schafer, Diane Stolen, Craig Heller, Walter Gutzmer, Buzz Brooks, Elsie Brooks.

APPENDIX 2. Artifacts Found at Little Rapids

	Field School Collections							Private Collections				Total
	ACT I	II	III	V	VI	OTHER	TOTAL	A	B	C	TOTAL	
HIDE-WORKING, CLOTHING-MANUFACTURE, AND REPAIR												
Tools:												
Iron awl	1	2				2	6	2	7	8	17	23
Bone handle		4					4	1	1		2	6
Bone flesher								1			1	1
Iron needle			1				1		2		2	3
Scissors			1				1		2	4	6	7
TOTAL	1	6	3			2	12	4	12	12	28	40
Cut-metal fragments:												
Brass	6	15	1		1	1	24	6	yes		>6	>30
Brass thimble		1					1					1
Sheet iron	24	48	6	2		9	91			>10	>10	>101
Iron kettle	14	35	5	2	1	8	63		2	>10	>12	>75
SILVER		1					1					1
TOTAL	44	100	12	2	4	18	180	6	>2	>20	>28	>218
Ornaments and Decoration												
Bells	4	4					8	2	3	2	7	15
Bracelets	1	1					2	1	2		3	5
Buckles									3	yes	>3	>3

Continued on next page

	Field School Collections							Private Collections				Total
	ACT I	II	III	V	VI	OTHER	TOTAL	A	B	C	TOTAL	
Buttons	6	3	3				12	9	3	5	17	29
Cowrie shell			1				1					1
Earrings	6	8	1		1		16	1			1	17
Glass beads	47	244	15	14	9	15	344	yes	13	yes	>13	>357
Hair ornament (kaolin)		1					1					1
Hook		1					1					1
Links	2	8				2	12					12
Mesh (silver)	1						1					1
Brooch (ring)	1	7	3				11	3	1		4	15
Brooch (round)	3	2	2				7		1	3	4	11
Rings		3					3		2	1	3	6
Tacks	6	6	4			1	17					17
Tinkling cones	19	28	7	2	5	3	64	6	4	4	14	78
Thimble (cut brass)	1						1					1
Wampum	3	10	1			1	15	yes	2		>2	>17
TOTAL	100	326	37	16	15	22	516	22	32	>17	>71	>587

FOOD PREPARATION
Kettle parts:

	Field School Collections							Private Collections				Total
Brass fragments							1		1		1	2
Iron chain		1							1		1	1
Iron fragments	27	16	1		3	5	52					52
Iron fragments (not cut)	23	8		1	16		48					48

Continued on next page

	Field School Collections							Private Collections				Total
	ACT I	II	III	V	VI	OTHER	TOTAL	A	B	C	TOTAL	
Bail fastener	1	1					2		2	3	5	7
Bail	1	1					2		1		1	3
Lug	1	2					3					3
TOTAL	53	29	1	1	3	21	108		5	3	8	116
Utensils:												
Spoons								2		2	4	4
HUNTING, TRAPPING, AND FISHING												
Fishhooks		1					1	2	11	8	21	22
Iron projectile points		1					1	1	8	13	22	23
Muskrat spear								3	3	17	23	23
Trap parts	1		1				2	2	8		10	12
Sinker										1	1	1
TOTAL	1	2	1				4	14	22	39	77	81
Gun parts:												
Barrel									4	4	8	8
Barrel tenon	1						1					1
Breech plug										1	1	1
Butt plate		1					1	2	4	2	8	9
Ferrule (rod guide)								1	2	2	5	5
Flintlock hammer			1				1	3	6	10	19	20
Frizzen								1	?	>1	>1	>1
Frizzen spring								3		3	3	3

Continued on next page

	Field School Collections							Private Collections				Total
	ACT I	II	III	V	VI	OTHER	TOTAL	A	B	C	TOTAL	
Gun bridle										6	6	6
Gun screw	1	1	1			1	4					4
Gun sight	2		1				3					3
Gun worm	1				1	1	2	yes	2		>2	>4
Gunstock pin								1			1	1
Jaw screw (vice)										10	10	10
Lock plate								3			3	3
Mainspring	1					1	2	2		10	12	14
Pan								1			1	1
Percussion cap			3				3					3
Sear			1				1	1		7	8	9
Sear spring		2					2	2		3	5	7
Side plate	1						1	1			1	2
Side plate (serpentine)	1		1				2	3	1	1	5	7
Trigger								3		8	11	11
Trigger guard			1				1	1	6	6	13	14
Tumbler										8	8	8
Tumbler screw	1						1					1
Wedge plate	1	1	1				3					3
TOTAL	9	5	9			3	28	28	25	78	131	159
Gunflints:												
British blade	1	3			2		6	8			8	14
Flakes	25	33	7		4	5	74					74
Fire flints	13	7	5		1		26					26

Continued on next page

	Field School Collections							Private Collections				Total
	ACT I	II	III	V	VI	OTHER	TOTAL	A	B	C	TOTAL	
French blade								1			1	1
Flakes	2	4	3			3	12					12
Fire flints		2	1			1	4					4
TOTAL	41	49	16		7	9	122	9			9	131
Lead Ammunition:												
Ball	3	2	1			1	7					
Buckshot	6	18	6			8	39					
Shot	5	70	3	5	1	10	94					
TOTAL	14	90	10	6	1	19	140	11	20	25	56	196
AMMUNITION MANUFACTURE												
Iron sieve	2	12					14	1	2	1	4	18
MISCELLANEOUS LEAD												
Modified	6	22	6		3	7	44					
Molds	2	9	4				15					
TOTAL	8	31	10		3	7	59	yes	yes	yes		>59
Lead Debris/Residue (Grams)	216	522	160	105	40.6	98.1	1141.7	192.8	yes	yes	>192.8	>1334.5
MULTIPURPOSE TOOLS												
Adze								1			1	1
Ax/hatchet								2	6	4	12	12

Continued on next page

	Field School Collections							Private Collections				Total
	ACT I	II	III	V	VI	OTHER	TOTAL	A	B	C	TOTAL	
Drill								1		1	1	1
File									2	3	6	6
Fire steel		1					1					1
Hoe								2	4	4	10	10
Knives	2	1				1	4	2	14	6	22	26
Nails (modified)	1	2					3					3
TOTAL	3	4				1	8	8	26	18	52	60
HARDWARE												
Hitching piece									1		1	1
Iron fragment (heavy)		5	2		7	1	15					15
Keyhole escutcheon		1					1	yes			>1	1
Latch/hinge								>12	1	>1	>1	>1
Nails (unmodified)	16	33			3	6	58	>12	>50	yes	>62	>120
Screws	2						2	1	yes	yes	1	3
Wire	5	4	2				11	5	yes	yes	>11	>11
TOTAL	23	43	4		10	7	87	>13	>52	yes	>65	>152
BONE ARTIFACTS												
Comb	1						1	1			1	1
Whistle		1					1					2
Modified bone	5	7					12					12
Antler	2	2					4					4
TOTAL	8	10					18	1			1	19

Continued on next page

	Field School Collections							Private Collections				Total
	ACT I	II	III	V	VI	OTHER	TOTAL	A	B	C	TOTAL	
PIPESTONE												
Disc	1						1					1
Flake/chip	11	58	6		3		78	7			7	85
Modified	2	6	2				10		1		1	11
Pipe fragment	7	6			2	2	17	8	1	1	10	27
TOTAL	21	70	8		5	2	106	16	1	1	18	124
LITHICS												
Chipped stone	493	129	758	6	384	488	2258					
Ground stone	4	1	2	1	3	2	13					
TOTAL	497	130	760	7	387	490	2271					2271
INDIAN CERAMICS	4	1	85	1	2	5	98	yes	yes			>98
GLASS												
Flat window:												
Light green	47	113	15		5	17	197					
Transparent	6	3					9					
TOTAL	53	116	15		5	17	206	yes	yes	yes		>206

Continued on next page

| | Field School Collections | | | | | | | Private Collections | | | | Total |
	ACT I	II	III	V	VI	OTHER	TOTAL	A	B	C	TOTAL	
Bottle:												
Amber						5	5					
Light green	3	16	1		1	4	25					
Olive	25	59	9		3	12	108					
Transparent	10	2	2			12	26					
TOTAL	38	77	12		4	33	164	yes	yes	yes		>164
Other:												
Melted					5		5					
Mirror	3						3					
TOTAL	46				5		51					51
EURO-AMERICAN CERAMICS	111	91	50		9	29	290	68	yes		>68	>358
KAOLIN PIPES Fragments	5	4	2			1	12	6			6	18

APPENDIX 3. Artifacts from Storage Pits near Lodge (Act I)

Pit Number	4	5	6	8	14	15	17	18	22	33	37	Total
FOOD PREPARATION												
Iron kettle fragment									1			1
CUT METAL												
Brass fragments							1					1
Iron fragments (cut sheet)				2	2							4
Iron kettle fragments									1			1
ORNAMENTS												
Glass beads	4		1	4	5			2				16
Bracelet (iron)								1				1
Brooch (silver round)	1											1
Button (iron)						1						1
Tack (brass)						1				1		2
Tinkling cone (iron)		1			1	1						3
Wampum					1							1
MULTI-PURPOSE TOOLS												
Knives						1						1
HARDWARE												
Nails (unmodified)			1	6								7
Screws				1								1
GUN PARTS												
Mainspring (iron)											1	1
Side plate (brass)				1								1
BRITISH BLADE GUNFLINTS												
Flakes	1				3	1	1					6
Fire flints			1					2				3

Continued on next page

Pit Number	4	5	6	8	14	15	17	18	22	33	37	Total
LEAD AMMUNITION												
Buckshot	1	1										2
Shot	2											2
MISCELLANEOUS LEAD												
Modified	1							1				2
BONE ARTIFACTS												
Comb				1								1
Modified bone				1								1
Antler						1						1
PIPESTONE												
Flake/chip		1				2						2
Pipe fragment		1		1								2
LITHICS												
Chipped stone		28	3	26	3	2	1	7			2	72
Ground stone											1	1
Modified		1		1	1							3
Rough rock			2		1							3
GLASS												
Flat window												
Light green		3	1		1	1	1	1				8
Bottle												
Light green		1		1								2
Transparent					2			1				3
Other												
Mirror										1		1
EURO-AMERICAN CERAMICS				1	1	1	1	4	1			8
TOTAL ARTIFACTS:	10	36	9	44	20	14	5	19	3	2	4	166
Lead Debris In Features (grams)		5.1	1.5	0.8	2.9	1.9		5.0				17.2

APPENDIX 4A: Animal Remains from Lodge Area (Act I)

Common Name	Species	Estimated individual vertebrates
Freshwater drumfish	*Aplodinotus grunniens*	21–30
River otter	*Lutra canadensis*	14–42
Muskrat	*Ondatra zibethicus*	7–29
Snapping turtle	*Chelydra serp.*	5–15
Painted turtle	*Chrysemys picta*	4–13
Deer	*Odocoileus sp.*	3–27
Wood duck	*Aix sponsa*	3–4
Soft-shell turtle	*Trionyx sp.*	2–10
Woodchuck	*Marmota monax*	2–6
Blanding's turtle	*Emys blandingi*	2–5
Blue-wing teal	*Anas discors*	2–5
Mallard duck	*Anas platyrhynchos*	2–4
Raccoon	*Procyon lotor*	2–4
Elk	*Cervus canadensis*	1–7
Shoveler duck	*Spatula clypeata*	1–3
Domestic pig	*Sus scrofa*	1–2
Dog, wolf, coyote	*Canis sp.*	1–2
Gar fish	*Lepisosteus sp.*	1
Redhead duck	*Aythya americana*	1
Vole	*Microtinae*	1
Passenger pigeon	*Ectopistes migratorius*	1
Bear	*Ursus americanus*	1
Lynx/bobcat	*Lynx sp.*	1
Pintail duck	*Anas acuta*	1
Badger	*Taxidea taxus*	1
Grebe (pied-billed)	*Podicipediidae sp.*	1
	TOTAL	82–217

NOTE: Numbers do not include animal remains from storage pits
(Whelan 1987)

APPENDIX 4B: Animal Remains from Community Dump (Act II)

Common Name	Species	Estimated individual vertebrates
Freshwater drumfish	*Aplodinotus grunniens*	91–95
Painted turtle	*Chrysemus picta*	21–34
Muskrat	*Ondatra zibethicus*	20–40
Woodchuck	*Marmota monax*	15–45

Common Name	Species	Estimated individual vertebrates
Passenger pigeon	*Ectopistes migratorius*	8–16
Deer	*Odocoileus* sp.	7–21
Blue-wing teal	*Anas discors*	7–17
Channel catfish	*Ictalurus punctatus*	7–11
Snapping turtle	*Chelydra serpentina*	6–24
Soft-shell turtle	*Trionyx* sp.	6–19
Walleye	*Stizostedion* sp.	5–8
Shoveler	*Spatula clypeata*	4–11
Dog, wolf, coyote	*Canis* sp.	4–10
Gar fish	*Lepisosteus* sp.	4–10
Mallard duck	*Anas platyrhynchos*	4–9
Blanding's turtle	*Emydoidia blandingi*	3–11
Wood duck	*Aix sponsa*	3–6
Northern pike/muskellunge	*Esox cf. lucius*	3–6
Flying squirrel	*Glaucomys* sp.	3–4
Flathead catfish	*Pylodictis olivaris*	3
Wood turtle	*Clemmys insculpta*	2–6
Redhead duck	*Aythya americana*	2–5
Coot	*Fulica americana*	2–5
Redhorse sucker	*Moxostoma* sp.	2–3
Merganser duck	*Mergus merganser*	2
Grouse	*Tetraonidae*	2
Rail	*Rallus* sp.	2
Elk	*Cervus canadensis*	1–7
Domestic pig	*Sus scrofa*	1–7
Raccoon	*Procyon lotor*	1–6
Grebe	*Podicipedidae*	1–4
Pintail duck	*Anas acuta*	1–3
River otter	*Lutra canadensis*	1–2
Common white sucker	*Catostomus commersoni*	1–2
Ruddy duck	*Oxyura jamaicensis*	1–2
Badger	*Taxidea taxus*	1–2
Bowfin	*Amia calva*	1
Woodpecker	*Podicipedidae*	1
Goose	*Branta canadensis*	1
Hawk	*Accipiter striatus*	1
Loon	*Gaviidae*	1
Map turtle	*Graptemys* sp.	1
	TOTAL	253–466

(Whelan 1987)

APPENDIX 5. Plant Remains

Common Name	
Bean family	Leguminosae
Corn*	*Zea mays*
Crabapple	*Cretagus* sp.
Cress family*	Crucifereae
Dandelion	*Taraxicum officinale*
Elderberry	*Sambucus* sp.
Grape*	*Vitis* sp.
Grass family	Gramineae (including *Pannicum* and *Setaria*)
Hazelnut*	*Corylus* sp.
Joe-pye weed*	*Eupatorium* sp.
Knotweed	*Polygonum* sp.
Mint family*	Labiatae
Motherwort	*Leonuvus cardiaca*
Nightshade	*Solanum dulcamara*
Pennycress	*Thalspi arvense*
Pig weed*	*Chenopodium*
Pin cherry or black cherry*	*Prunus pennsylvanica* or *serotina*
Plantain	*Plantago major*
Potato family*	*Solanum* [*Solanum tuberosum?* Solanaceae?]
Purslane*	*Portulaca oleraceae*
Ragweed	*Ambrosia* (including *Ambrosia artemisifolia*)
Raspberry	*Rubus* sp.
Sedge family*	Cyperaceae (including *Carex* and *Scirpus*)
Sorrell	*Oxalis stricta*
Spurge	*Euphorbia* sp.
Staghorn sumac	*Rhus* sp.
Strawberry*	*Fragaria vesca*
Vervain	*Verbena bracteata*
Wild cherry*	*Prunus americana*

*Charred
(Shane 1984)

SOURCES

Albert, Alphaeus H.

1973   Record of American uniform and historical buttons, with supplement, 1775–1973. Boyertown, Pa.: Boyertown Publishing Company.

Anderson, Gary C.

1984   Kinsmen of another kind: Dakota-White relations in the upper Mississippi valley, 1650–1862. Lincoln: University of Nebraska Press.

Anfinson, Scott F.

1984   Cultural and natural aspects of mound distribution in Minnesota. Minnesota Archaeologist 43 (no. 1):3–30.

Babcock, Willoughby M.

1945   Sioux villages in Minnesota prior to 1837. Minnesota Archaeologist 11 (no. 1):126–46.

Binford, Lewis R.

1980   Willow smoke and dogs' tails: Hunter-gatherer settlement systems and archaeological site formation. American Antiquity 45 (no. 1):4–20.

Black Thunder, Elijah, Norma Johnson, Larry O'Connor, and Muriel Pronovost

1975   Ehanna woyakapi: History and culture of the Sisseton-Wahpeton Sioux tribe of South Dakota. Sisseton: Sisseton-Wahpeton Tribe.

Blakey, Michael

1983   Socio-political bias and ideological production in historical archaeology. In The socio-politics of archaeology. Research report no. 23, 5–16. Amherst: Department of Anthropology, University of Massachusetts.

Bray, Edmund C., and Martha C. Bray, trans. and eds.

1976   *Joseph N. Nicollet on the plains and prairies. The expeditions of 1838–39 with journals, letters, and notes on the Dakota Indians.* St. Paul: Minnesota Historical Society Press.

Brown, Ralph D.

1937   Report of a visit to a site which may prove to be that of J. B. Faribault's trading post near Chaska. Typescript. Minnesota Historical Society Archives, History Center, St. Paul (hereafter MHS).

Brown, Jennifer S.

1980   *Strangers in blood. Fur trade company families in Indian country.* Vancouver: University of British Columbia Press.

Cavender, Chris C.

1986a   The Oceti Sakowin (seven council fires). Field school program, July 1, 1986. Typescript. Department of Anthropology, University of Minnesota, Minneapolis (hereafter UM).

1986b   The Dakota communities of Minnesota. Field school program, July 2, 1986. Typescript. Department of Anthropology, UM.

1986c   Dakota place names. Field school program, July 3, 1986. Typescript. Department of Anthropology, UM.

1986d   The Dakota mind: Religious thought and philosophy. Field school program, July 8–15, 1986. Typescript. Department of Anthropology, UM.

1986e   The Dakota family. Field school program, July 16–17, 1986. Typescript. Department of Anthropology, UM.

Clifford, James L., and George E. Marcus, eds.

1986   *Writing culture: The poetics and politics of ethnography.* Berkeley: University of California Press.

Conkey, Margaret W., and Janet D. Spector

1984   Archaeology and the study of gender. *Advances in Archaeological Method and Theory* 7:1–38.

Cushing, Edward U.

1986   Vegetation at the Little Rapids site, Scott Co. Minnesota. Field school program. Typescript. Department of Anthropology, UM.

Deloria, Vine, Jr.

1989   A simple question of humanity: The moral dimensions of the reburial issue. *Legal Review* 14 (no. 4):1–12.

Densmore, Frances

1954   *The collection of water-color drawings of the North American Indian by Seth Eastman.* St. Paul: James Jerome Hill Reference Library.

Eastman, Charles A.

[1902] *Indian boyhood.* New York: Dover Publications, Inc.
1971

Eastman, Mary H.
   1853   *The American aboriginal portfolio.* Philadelphia: Lippincott, Grambo and
        Company.

Eclov, Timothy
   1981   Gunflints and gun parts from the Little Rapids site. Typescript. Depart-
        ment of Anthropology, UM.

Faribault, Jean B.
   1833   Invo. of sundry merchandise furnished Jean Bt. Farribault for the trade
        of the Little Rapids since the 27th November 1832 up to June 1833.
        Vol. 60, Alexis Bailly Papers. MHS.

Feder, Norman
   1964   *Art of the eastern Plains Indians. The Nathan Sturges Jarvis collection.*
        Brooklyn: The Brooklyn Museum.

Fernald, Merritt L.
   1970   *Gray's manual of botany.* 8th ed. New York: Van Nostrand Reinhold
        Company.

Folwell, William W.
   [1921] *A history of Minnesota.* Vol. 1. St. Paul: Minnesota Historical Society.
   1956

Freeman, Joan E.
   1986   Aztalan: A middle Mississippian village. *Introduction to Wisconsin Ar-
        chaeology,* edited by William Green, James B. Stoltman, and Alice Kehoe.
        Special issue. *The Wisconsin Archaeologist* 67(nos. 3–4):339–64.

Furst, Randy
   1992   3,000 Indians, supporters denounce mascot names. *Minneapolis Star
        Tribune,* Jan. 2, 1992, p. 11A.

Gero, Joan M.
   1983   Gender bias in archaeology: A cross-cultural perspective. In *The socio-
        politics of archaeology,* edited by Joan M. Gero, David M. Lacy, Michael L.
        Blakey. Research report no. 23, 51–57. Amherst: Department of An-
        thropology, University of Massachusetts.

Gilman, Rhoda R.
   1970   Last days of the upper Mississippi fur trade. *Minnesota History* 42
        (no. 4):123–40.

Gurnoe, Donald G.
   1980   Letter to Norman Crooks, April 7, 1980, Department of Anthropology,
        UM.

Gustafson, Mary Jane
   1972   He discovers Jean Faribault's fur trading post. *North Minneapolis Post,*
        Nov. 9, 1972, p. A9.

Halloran, Teresa
   1982   Photographic inventory of collections from Little Rapids. Typescript.
           Department of Anthropology, UM.

Hanson, Charles E., Jr.
   1955   *The northwest gun.* Publications in anthropology no. 2. Lincoln: Nebraska
           State Historical Society.

Hassrick, Royal B.
   1964   *The Sioux: Life and customs of a warrior society.* Norman: University of
           Oklahoma Press.

Henderson, Mae
   1990   History, narrative, metaphor and the construction of subjectivity in Toni
           Morrison's *Beloved.* Paper presented at the Center For Advanced
           Feminist Studies, University of Minnesota, Minneapolis, April 16, 1990.

Hodder, Ian
   1989   Writing archaeology: Site reports in context. *Antiquity* 63:268–74.

Holcombe, Return I., and William H. Bingham, eds.
   1915   *Compendium of history and biography of Carver and Hennepin counties, Min-
           nesota.* Chicago: Henry Taylor & Co.

Hughes, Thomas
   [1927] *Indian Chiefs of Southern Minnesota.* Minneapolis: Ross and Haines.
   1969

Johnson, Richard
   1990   The bones of their fathers. *Sunday Denver Post,* Feb. 4, 1990, Contem-
           porary sec., 13–21.

Jones, Olive R.
   1981   Essence of peppermint, a history of the medicine and its bottle. *Historical
           Archaeology* 15 (no. 2):16–21.

Keyes, Charles R.
   1928   The Hill-Lewis archaeological survey. *Minnesota History* 9 (no. 2):96–108.

Klammer, Paul W.
   1935   What a find. *Minnesota Archaeologist* 1 (no. 2):3–5.

Klammer, K. K., and Paul W. Klammer
   1949   The Little Rapids trading post. *Minnesota Archaeologist* 15 (no .2):30–57.

La Bathe, François
   1828   Invoice of goods in charge of François La Bathe to trade at the Little
           Rapids. Vol. 23, box 5, Alexis Bailly Papers. MHS.

Lofstrom, Edward U.
   1976   An analysis of temporal change in a 19th-century ceramic assemblage
           from Fort Snelling, Minnesota. *Minnesota Archaeologist* 35 (no. 1):16–47.

Markoe, Glenn E., ed.
   1986   *Vestiges of a proud nation: The Ogden B. Read northern Plains Indian collec-
           tion.* Burlington, Vt.: Robert Hull Fleming Museum.

Martin, Alexander C., and William D. Barkley

  1961   *Seed identification manual.* Berkeley and Los Angeles: University of California Press.

Mascia-Lees, Frances, Patricia Sharpe, and Colleen Cohen

  1989   The postmodernist turn in anthropology: Cautions from a feminist perspective. *Signs: Journal of Women in Culture and Society* 15 (no. 11):7–33.

Mason, Ronald J.

  1986   *Rock Island: Historical Indian archaeology in the northern Lake Michigan basin.* Midcontinental Journal of Archaeology Special Paper no. 6. Kent, Ohio: Kent State University Press.

Mbilinyi, Marjorie

  1989   "I'd have been a man": Politics and the labor process in producing personal narratives. In *Interpreting women's lives: Feminist theory and personal narratives,* edited by Personal Narratives Group, 204–27. Bloomington: Indiana University Press.

McDermott, John F.

  1961   *Seth Eastman: Pictorial historian of the Indian.* Norman: University of Oklahoma Press.

  1973   *Seth Eastman's Mississippi: A lost portfolio recovered.* Urbana: University of Illinois Press.

McLaughlin, Marie L.

  [1916]   *Myths and legends of the Sioux.* Lincoln: University of Nebraska Press.
  1990

McNickle, D'Arcy

  1972   American Indians who never were. In *The American Indian reader: Anthropology,* edited by Jeannette Henry, 29–36. San Franciso: Indian Historian Press.

Medicine, Bea, Alfonso Ortiz, and D'Arcy McNickle

  1972   The anthropologist: The man and the discipline. In *The American Indian reader: Anthropology,* edited by Jeannette Henry, 1–3. San Francisco: Indian Historical Press.

Meyer, Roy W.

  1967   *History of the Santee Sioux: United States Indian policy on trial.* Lincoln: University of Nebraska Press.

(MHS) Minnesota Historical Society

  1977   Little Rapids. Minnesota archaeological site file (21SC27), Scott County. Typescript. State Historic Preservation Office, MHS.

  n.d.   Little Rapids trading post, Scott County, Minnesota. Typescript. State Historic Preservation Office, MHS.

Minnich, Elizabeth

  1982   A devastating conceptual error: How can we not be feminist scholars?" *Change Magazine* 14 (April):7–9.

Monroe, Dan L., and Walter Echo-Hawk
  1991   Deft deliberations. *Museum News* 70 (no. 4):55–58.
Moore, Henrietta L.
  1988   *Feminism and anthropology*. Minneapolis: University of Minnesota Press.
Moore, Stephen
  1989   Federal Indian burial policy: Historical anachronism or contemporary reality?" In *Conflict in the archaeology of living traditions,* edited by R. Layton, 201–10. London: Unwin Hyman.
Morgen, Sandra, ed.
  1989   *Gender and anthropology: Critical reviews for research and teaching.* Washington, D.C.: American Anthropological Association.
Morrison, Toni
  1987   Site of memory. In *Inventing the truth: The art and craft of memoir,* edited by William Zinsser, 101–24. Boston: Houghton Mifflin Company.
Neill, Edward D.
  1858   *The history of Minnesota: From the earliest French explorations to the present time*. Philadelphia: J. B. Lippincott & Co.
Parker, Donald D.
  1966   *The recollections of Philander Prescott: Frontiersman of the old Northwest, 1819–1862.* Lincoln: University of Nebraska Press.
Pond, Samuel W.
 [1908]   *The Dakota or Sioux in Minnesota as they were in 1834.* St. Paul: Minnesota
  1986   Historical Society.
Prescott, Philander
  1852   Contributions to the history, customs, and opinions of the Dacota tribe.
  1853   In *Information respecting the history, condition and prospects of the Indian tribes of the United States,* edited by Henry Schoolcraft, 2:168–99, 3:225–46. Philadelphia: Lippincott, Grambo and Company.
  1854   Manners, customs, and opinions of the Dacotahs. In *Information respecting the history, condition and prospects of the Indian tribes of the United States,* edited by Henry Schoolcraft, 4:59–72. Philadelphia: Lippincott, Grambo and Company.
Quimby, George I.
  1966   *Indian culture and European trade goods.* Madison: University of Wisconsin Press.
Riggs, Stephen R.
  1869   *Táh-koo Wah-kán; or the gospel among the Dakotas.* Boston: Congregational Sabbath-School and Publishing Society.
 [1880]   *Mary and I: Forty years with the Sioux.* Minneapolis: Ross and Haines.
  1969
  1890   A Dakota-English dictionary. In *Contributions to North American ethnology*. Vol. 7. Washington, D.C.: Government Printing Office.

1893   Dakota grammar, texts, and ethnography. In *Contributions to North American ethnology*. Vol. 9. Washington, D.C.: Government Printing Office.

Rosaldo, Michelle Z.

1980   The use and abuse of anthropology: Reflections on feminism and cross-cultural understanding. *Signs: Journal of Women in Culture and Society 5* (no. 3):389–417.

Rosaldo, Renato

1986   Where objectivity lies: The rhetoric of anthropology. Paper presented at the University of Minnesota, Minneapolis, Feb. 27, 1986.

1989   *Culture and truth: The remaking of social analysis*. Boston: Beacon Press.

Schiffer, Michael B.

1976   *Behavioral archaeology*. New York: Academic Press.

Schommer, Carolynn I.

1986   Dakota-language study sheets. Field school program. Typescript. Department of Anthropology, UM.

Schoolcraft, Henry R.

1853   Sioux population in 1836. In *Information respecting the history, condition and prospects of the Indian tribes of the United States,* edited by Henry Schoolcraft, 3:612. Philadelphia: Lippincott, Grambo and Company.

Sibley, Henry H.

1880   Memoir of Jean Baptiste Faribault. *Collections of the Minnesota Historical Society* 3:168–79. St. Paul: Minnesota Historical Society.

Shane, Linda C. K.

1984   Seed analysis: Little Rapids site (21Sc27). Typescript. Department of Anthropology, UM.

Skinner, Alanson B.

1920   Medicine ceremony of the Menomini, Iowa, and Wahpeton Dakota, with notes on the ceremony among the Ponca, Bungi Ojibwa, and Potawatomi. In *Indian notes and monographs*. Vol. 4. New York: Museum of the American Indian.

Sletto, Jacqueline W.

1992   Pipestone. *Native Peoples* 5 (Winter):20–24.

South, Stanley A.

1978   Evolution and horizon as revealed in ceramic analysis in historical archaeology. Reprinted in *Historical archaeology: A guide to substantive and theoretical contributions,* edited by Robert L. Schuyler, 68–82. Farmingdale, NY: Baywood Pubishing Company.

Spector, Janet D.

1970   Seed analysis in archaeology. *Wisconsin Archaeologist* 51 (no. 4):163–90.

1974   *Prehistoric midwestern woodland Indians*. Fort Atkinson, Wi.: NASCO.

1975   Crabapple Point (Je93): An historic Winnebago Indian site in Jefferson County, Wisconsin. *Wisconsin Archaeologist* 56 (no. 4):270–345.

1978   The interpretive potential of glass trade beads in historic archaeology. *Historical Archaeology* 10:17–27.

1983   Male/female task differentiation among the Hidatsa: Toward the development of an archaeological approach to the study of gender. In *The hidden half,* edited by Patricia Albers and Beatrice Medicine, 77–99. Washington, D.C.: University Press of America.

1985   Ethnoarchaeology and Little Rapids: A new approach to 19th century Eastern Dakota sites. In *Archaeology, ecology, and ethnohistory of the prairie-forest border zone of Minnesota and Manitoba,* edited by J. Spector and E. Johnson, 167–203. Lincoln: J & L Reprint Company.

Spector, Janet D., and Mary K. Whelan
1989   Incorporating gender into archaeology courses. In *Gender and anthropology: Critical reviews for research and teaching,* edited by Sandra Morgen, 65–94. Washington, D.C.: American Anthropological Association.

Sprague, Roderick
n.d.   Glass beads from the Black Dog burial site (21 DK 26). Typescript. Archaeology Department, MHS.

Stolen, Diane M.
1988   Little Rapids: A map portrait of an 1830s Dakota village. Typescript. Department of Anthropology, UM.

Stone, Lyle M.
1974   *Fort Michilimackinac 1715-1781: An archaeological perspective on the revolutionary frontier.* East Lansing: Publications of the Museum, Michigan State University.

Taliaferro, Lawrence
1826   Letter to Robert Stuart, April 2, 1826. Letters received by the Office of Indian Affairs, St. Peter's Agency, Records of the Bureau of Indian Affairs, record number 75, roll 757, National Archives.

1839   Report of Lawrence Taliaferro, agent at St. Peters. 26th Cong., 1 sess., House Document, no. 2, 493–98. Serial 363.

Tanner, Helen H., ed.
1987   *Atlas of Great Lakes Indian history.* Norman: University of Oklahoma Press.

Trigger, Bruce G.
1980   Archaeology and the image of the American Indian. *American Antiquity* 45 (no. 4):662–76.

(UM) University of Minnesota
1975   Survey sheet, Scott County (21Sc27). Typescript. Archaeological Laboratory, Department of Anthropology, UM.

(USFWS) U.S. Fish and Wildlife Service

1982   *Minnesota Valley National Wildlife Refuge—Final environmental impact statement.* Department of the Interior. St. Paul: U.S. Fish and Wildlife Service.

n.d.   *Minnesota Valley National Wildlife Refuge, recreation area, and state trail.* Brochure, n.p. St. Paul: U.S. Fish and Wildlife Service.

Van Kirk, Sylvia

1980   *"Many tender ties": Women in fur-trade society in western Canada, 1670-1870.* Winnipeg, Manitoba: Watson & Dwyer Publishing Ltd.

Wallace, Michael D.

1981   Visiting the past: History museums in the United States. *Radical History Review* 25:63–96.

Walsh, Henry B.

1854   Land survey notes and map, Louisville Township, Scott County, Minnesota. MS, Secretary of State files, State Office Building, St. Paul, Minnesota.

Whelan, Mary K.

1987   *The archaeological analysis of a* 19th century Dakota economy. Ph.D. diss. Department of Anthropology, UM.

Wilford, Lloyd A.

1941   Memoranda on Scott County. Typescripts. Department of An-
1951   thropology, UM.

1952

1956

1957

Willey, Gordon R., and Jeremy A. Sabloff

1974   *A history of American archaeology.* San Francisco: W. H. Freeman and Company.

Williamson, John P., comp.

[1902]   *An English-Dakota dictionary. Wasicum ka Dakota ieska wowapi.* Min-
1970   neapolis: Ross & Haines, Inc.

Williamson, Thomas S.

1851   Dacotas of the Mississippi. In *Information respecting the history, condition and prospects of the Indian tribes of the United States,* edited by Henry Schoolcraft, 1:247–56. Philadelphia: Lippincott, Grambo and Company.

Winchell, Newton H.

1911   *The aborigines of Minnesota.* St. Paul: Minnesota Historical Society.

Withrow, Randall M.

1989a   Inventory of datable items, Little Rapids site (21Sc27). Typescript. Department of Anthropology, UM.

1989b   Notes on the geology of Little Rapids. Typescript. Department of Anthropology, UM.

1989c A report on soil-probe testing of the earthen enclosure at the Little Rapids site. Typescript. Department of Anthropology, UM.

Woolworth, Alan R., and Nancy L. Woolworth

1980 Eastern Dakota settlement and subsistence patterns prior to 1851. *Minnesota Archaeologist* 39 (no. 2): 70–89.

Zimmerman, Larry J.

1989 Human bones as symbols of power: Aboriginal American belief systems toward bones and "grave-robbing" archaeologists. In *Conflict in the archaeology of living traditions,* edited by R. Layton, 211–16. London: Unwin Hyman.

INDEX

Agriculture, relation to gender roles, 49, 109–10; summer planting, 76–77

American Fur Company, trade goods, 63; post, 65; traders, 123

Animal remains, excavated, 93, 104–5, 107, 109, 112–13, 143–44 (appendix 4); depicted, 104

Anptuxa (Red Day), 43

Anthropology, feminist, 33; cultural, 34; impact on digs, 57

Archaeologists, characterized, 30

Archaeology, education and training, 1–6, 35, 61–62, 85, 91; digs by amateurs, 14, 58–60, 82, 86, 122, 125; methodology, 30–31, 65; cultural bias discussed, 31–32; gender bias discussed, 32–33; traditional reports, 33; theories about mounds, 54–56; protection of sites, 56–57; fraud discovered, 60; as drama, 79; excavation methods, 87, 89–92, 95, 98; excavation depicted, 90, 99, 100, 104; ethical aspect, 122. *See also* Feminist archaeology

Artifacts, excavated, 35, 58, 93, 94–95, 98, 104–5, 106–9, 114–16, 120, 123–25; trade goods, 63, 86–87; trade goods depicted, 64, 115; from test pits, 83; listed, 96, 133–42 (appendixes 2 and 3); depicted, 97, 122, 124

Ashley, Edward, missionary, 56

Awl, described, 23, 25; lost, 27, 29; case depicted, 28; as trade item, 30, 31; depicted, 32; in traditional archaeological context, 33; found, 105

Awl handle, described, 18; depicted, 22, 36; discovered, 35; inscriptions described, 36–37

Aztalan, Wis., dig, 3

Bailly, Alexis, trader, 64

Beadwork, depicted, 23, 24, 28; described, 106

Bellecourt, Clyde, leader, 127

Binford, Lewis, archaeologist, 12

Bingham, William H., historian, 46

Black Thunder, Elijah, historian, 37, 49, 112

FIG. 1, Alan Ominsky, Minnesota Historical Society (hereafter MHS), based on Tanner 1987, map 28; figs. 2, 13, 33–35, 38–41, 44, 47, Janet D. Spector; figs. 3, 9, 16 (photographed by Monroe P. Killy), 17, 18 (Riggs 1880), MHS collections; figs. 4, 10, James J. Hill Reference Library, St. Paul; figs. 5, 6 (from Rose Bluestone family), 11, Arlo Hasse collection, Cologne (photographed by Diane M. Stolen); figs. 7, 8, 12, 14, 23 (Klammers and University of Minnesota collections), 36–37, 42, 43, 45–46, Diane M. Stolen; fig. 15, Smithsonian Institution, Washington, D.C.; fig. 19, Scott County Recorder's Office, Chaska; fig. 20, Winchell 1911, 191; fig. 21, Klammer and Klammer 1949, 32; fig. 22, Bailly papers, vol. 20, MHS; figs. 24–31, M. Eastman 1853, 51, 73, 39, 63, 55, 75, 58, 41; fig. 32, U.S. Department of Agriculture. All artifact and site photographs are in the University of Minnesota collections.

About the Seth Eastman figures:

Seth Eastman was stationed in the army at Fort Snelling from 1830 to 1831 and again from 1841 to 1848. During these years and into the mid-1850's, he produced many dozens of pencil sketches, watercolor drawings, and oil paintings depicting the life and culture of the area's Dakota residents. Eastman also made sketches that he frequently copied and recopied in other mediums, sometimes slightly modifying his composition. Exact dates cannot be assigned to these works.

In addition, Eastman produced a number of watercolors to appear as plates in editor Henry Rowe Schoolcraft's multivolume *Historical and Statistical Information Respecting the History, Condition and Prospects of the Indian Tribes of the United States* (Philadelphia: Lippincott, Grambo and Company), published between 1851 and 1857. Eastman works were also copied by engravers and lithographers for several publications written and assembled by Eastman's wife, Mary. The engravings reproduced in *What This Awl Means* appeared in *The American Aboriginal Portfolio* (Philadelphia: Lippincott, Grambo and Company), issued in 1853.

For more information on Eastman, readers are referred to John Francis McDermott's *Seth Eastman, Pictorial Historian of the Indian* (Norman: University of Oklahoma Press, 1961).

JANET D. SPECTOR is professor emerita of anthropology at the University of Minnesota. She has received several awards for distinguished teaching.

Photograph by Tom Foley, University of Minnesota

Printed in the USA
CPSIA information can be obtained
at www.ICGtesting.com
JSHW052017140824
68134JS00027B/2524

9 780873 512787